REFLECTIONS

ON LEADERSHIP

REFLECTIONS
ON LEADERSHIP

MY LIFE EXPERIENCES

G JAGANNATHAN

STRIKING**IDEAS**

PUBLISHED BY — STRIKING IDEAS LLC — UNITED STATES OF AMERICA

Dedicated at the lotus feet
of my guru, guide, and god, Sri Sathya Sai Baba

First Edition: 2021

ISBN 9798778533660

Copyright © 2021 — G Jagannathan

PUBLISHED BY — STRIKING IDEAS LLC
UNITED STATES OF AMERICA

An inspiration to shape oneself,
ushering change from within, to serve with devotion and selflessness

CONTENTS

Lineage nor patronage,

Position nor power,

Region nor religion,

Style nor sect,

Colour nor country,

None describe leaders.

What they think,

What they say,

What they do, reveals

Who they truly are!

— G Jagannathan

Foreword by Raja Krishnamoorthi

Member of Congress, United States House of Representatives

We live in fractious times. Social media, which announced itself as a bridge to build friendships and connect the world, now divides our body politic and amplifies some of our worst impulses. People speak without irony about the importance of building a *"brand of me"*, as though our personal achievements were the result of a singular effort. We seem to have lost our capacity to appreciate that each of us benefits from the support and guidance of a network of colleagues and mentors, and the access to information we enjoy in our interconnected, technologically advanced 21st-century world.

We need leaders who can articulate a shared vision that binds us together, whose words and deeds provide a common inspiration to build a better world for ourselves, for our children, and for our children's children.

This is why Reflections on Leadership is so timely. The lessons in Govindarajan Jagannathan's book are drawn from his experience as a senior manager with the Tata Group — one of the world's largest and most successful global enterprises. Jagannathan has distilled his life's work into a primer on building a culture of leadership that supports business excellence and the pursuit of that excellence with integrity and a sense of social responsibility. Through vignettes gleaned from work experiences and personal contact with exceptional leaders in business and government, and through historical and spiritual references, Jagannathan articulates a pathway to values-driven leadership that also is informed by his deeply held spiritual beliefs. His leadership *dharma* eschews individual aggrandisement and demands a profound humility and commitment to serving others and is grounded in the core belief that only through the coordinated efforts of many can great accomplishments be realised.

We need more leaders with heart. This book will help illuminate their path.

Raja Krishnamoorthi
Member of Congress
US House of Representatives

October 20, 2021

Prologue by Arun M Kumar

Chairman and CEO, KPMG in India

Socrates said the unexamined life is not worth living. In Reflections on Leadership: my life experiences, G Jagannathan contemplates his rich experiences to provide coherent perspectives on the complex question of what constitutes inspiring and authentic leadership.

Indeed, in an era when a discontinuity is the only constant, the ability to lead wisely is prized. The business, political and social worlds today yearn for authentic leadership. Authenticity reflects aspects of the leader's inner self.

Every great leader's journey is informed by self-reflection on the kind of person they want to be. All change must start from within. The nuanced lessons in Jaggu's book draw on his many years of leading teams, and in particular creating value through his innate passion for excellence and learning.

As you read this book, you will not fail to notice the many examples presented in the carefully crafted sections – on each of the pillars of Humility, Excellence, Action, Respect and Teamwork, constituting a well-coined acronym HEART. These elements represent the hallmarks of genuine, consistent, and versatile leadership.

What struck me equally was the profound conclusion in the final chapter of the book, *"Deep Within"*, where the author narrates his firm beliefs on the 'gold standard' of leadership — inspirational leadership, lived through example, driven by living one's values every day.

Jaggu's experiences and writing highlight the special qualities of inspiring leaders. These leaders have the humility, courage, and insight to benefit from the expertise of those who have less power than them. They actively seek to create an environment of learning and display openness to ideas.

I was reminded of Mahatma Gandhi's leadership principles. He used the power of humility and respect to win over others. In the Mahatma's words, *"The first condition of humaneness is a little humility and a little diffidence about the correctness of one's conduct and a little receptiveness."*

This book shares rich experiences in an honest manner as it raises reflective questions and provides purposeful lessons.

Arun M Kumar

Chairman and CEO, KPMG in India

November 1, 2021

Introduction by Dr. R. Balasubramaniam

Founder of Swami Vivekananda Youth Movement,
Member HR Capacity Building Commission, Government of India

G eorges Braque, the art critic, had this to say about art – *"There is only one valuable thing in art: the thing you cannot explain."* Leadership, like art, is another very difficult thing to explain but is very valuable for humankind. Whether it is the corporate CEO, or the NGO leader, the politician, or the man on the street, every one of us is affected both by leadership and the lack of it. Studying it has been the pursuit of several people around the world and it is also one of the most published subjects of our times. G Jagannathan's book, Reflections on Leadership is the answer for those who will wonder if another book makes a difference.

Jaggu, as the author is fondly known, does not claim to be a leadership expert or an academic devoted to research in this field. While he has held several leadership positions and worked in several countries, he brings the unique combination of being a practitioner himself, but with a ringside view of how leaders at very high levels think and operate. Combining the knowledge of the civilization wisdom of India with experiential insights, he has produced this wonderful book on leadership, which is everyday practice embedded in leadership theory.

The domination of western thought in leadership literature gives the impression that other countries may have little to offer. Ancient civilizations like India are replete with numerous principles of leadership hidden in the rich scriptural and puranic traditions of the land. Unpacking them needs both an understanding of the Indian milieu and the ability to connect them to the current leadership context. Jaggu does this with neither undue romanticisation nor misplaced humility and the list of takeaways presented at the end of each chapter is testimony to this ability of his.

The discussions on who is a leader or what constitutes leadership is an ongoing one. Whether a person is a born leader or gets made into one is another argument that has been around for ages. I believe that it is all about exercising leadership and not about 'being or becoming a leader'. This abstraction is not easy to deconstruct and make meaning of unless we see it manifested by the people exercising them. Jaggu draws examples of persons from history *(both recent and remote),* from his own personal and professional spaces and gives us illustrations of people who are not just role models for society but are great exemplifiers of leadership in different domains of work.

The quality of humility is foundational for the exercise of leadership. From being the basis for lifelong learning to helping one come to terms with one's own vulnerability, humility is critical in the journey of subsuming one's ego. The ongoing COVID crisis has shown us how fragile and vulnerable human existence is. It also demonstrated how those with the humility to learn from and work with others were the ones who helped provide hope. Many of them presented the several qualities that Jaggu describes in the book, offering us the evidence that his examples are not merely anecdotal but form the basis of leadership paradigms.

Whether it is the urge to excel, or staying focused on the work at the centre rather than on oneself, leading ethically, to paying attention to the minutest detail – it is all well-articulated by Jaggu. Drawing inspiration from the house of Tata's, he shares several stories that are not in the public domain. Anecdotes involving Russi Mody, JRD Tata, Ratan Tata, Ramadorai and Chandra are woven in seamlessly. While the reflections are based on his own personal experiences, it is only natural that we see his skew towards the Tata legacy. Being a TATA scholar and associated with the Tata group for a long time now, I can vouch for the several examples of ethics, excellence, compassion, humility and the spirit of egalitarianism that he writes about.

Swami Vivekananda gave a call to the youth of India to follow the '3H' mantra all our lives. He spoke on how critical it was to have the 'HEART to feel', the 'HEAD to think' and the 'HANDS to act'. In a subtle manner, Swamiji embedded the leadership principles of Motivation (Heart), Strategy (Head) and Action (Hands) into his national message. He saw the need for all his devotees to base their everyday actions on the '3 Ps' - Purity, Patience and Perseverance. This book serves to remind us of these cardinal leadership principles, and Jaggu has done well to bring them out through his thoughts on great personalities and his own experiences with them.

From Cricket to Singapore Airlines, from Gandhi to Mother Teresa, from President Kalam to Bhagwan Sathya Sai Baba, this book, rich in anecdotes, is practical in its approach, and pragmatic in the leadership message. This book is not for any one single audience and will resonate with both young and old alike, with practitioners and academicians and with all those who desire to make a difference in their lives. One may choose to read this book in one go, or savour it as I did over several days, or revisit it regularly – whatever one chooses to do, one surely needs to pause after each section, reflect and use the takeaways to inspire ourselves on the need for and importance of exercising leadership both in our personal and professional lives.

Jaggu's book is driven by personal spiritual longings and will help all those who see the exercise of leadership as a lifelong sadhana. Each day provides us with opportunities to evolve, to make ourselves a little better and fitter to exercise the leadership to make this world a better place. Reflections on Leadership comes at a time when each one of us needs this reminder on a regular basis, and I am sure that there will be several like me who will make this book a daily read.

Dr. R. Balasubramaniam
Founder of Swami Vivekananda Youth Movement,
Member HR Capacity Building
October 20, 2021 *Commission, Government of India*

Acknowledgements

I am indebted to so many!

This book is made possible by the active role played by many scholars and well-wishers, whom I would like to acknowledge. They shared their thoughts, insights, and most notably, their valuable time with practical ideas. This list includes successful authors, practitioners, CXOs, academic scholars, young managers, budding leaders, and artists. Without their encouragement and critical but constructive criticism, the book would not have taken its current shape.

Many leaders weave the fabric of human development from the realms of politics, business, and the community at large. They usher economic progress, make a difference at the grassroots level, and alter the trajectory for prosperity, all-around peace, and well-being. We are blessed to have all three voices to grace this book.

Raja Krishnamoorthi, a member of Congress in the United States House of Representatives, is one of the top leaders. The subject of Leadership Reflections is common ground that we share. I express my thankfulness to Raja Krishnamoorthi for agreeing to write the Foreword in my book and extend his influence on the aspiring leaders of tomorrow. Thank you, Raja, for the context that you have set.

I wish to express my deepest gratitude to Arun M Kumar, Chairman and CEO, KPMG in India, as a senior commercial diplomat and acclaimed business leader with vast experience in leading business prosperity. He brings his most relevant and rich observations in writing the Prologue and elaborates that a great leader's journey begins with self-reflection. Thank you, Arun, for your pearls of wisdom.

I am deeply touched and humbled by the Introduction by Dr. R. Balasubramaniam, Founder of Swami Vivekananda Youth Movement, and Member HR Capacity Building Commission, Government of India, for a captivating rendition that has touched many facets elaborated in the book. The depth of his reflections is fascinating. Thank you, Dr. R. Balasubramaniam, for gracing us with your detailed articulation.

I am thankful to Raghu Kalé, my friend, colleague, author, scriptwriter, editor, video film producer, publisher, and long-time senior executive of some of the world-class companies of the Tata Group, and currently the Founder and CEO of Striking Ideas for motivating and encouraging me to share my experience of four decades on the subject. He made a schedule and strictly followed the military discipline for reviews that lasted more than a year. Special thanks to him for the cover design, insights on several chapters, and for setting up the resources to publish this book.

I am grateful to Dr. Shashank Shah, JN Tata Scholar 2015, Harvard Business School; SAI Fellow 2017, Harvard University; author of several books; Top 200 Global Thought Leader; and keynote speaker, who readily agreed to review and edit this book with humility. He provided deep insights, especially on the last chapter titled "It Is Deep Within". His cheerful and wholehearted participation boosted my energy and helped me correct and perfect in many ways. My sincere thanks to this young but professional research scholar. The best part is he did everything with a smile.

Thanks to Ms. Usha Rangarajan *(Founder and Managing Consultant, UnLeash)*, Sunil Kasturi *(Chief Growth Officer, Propeller),* D Rangarao *(Value Management and Supply-Chain Consultant)*, and Ritesh Reddy *(Senior Software Consultant, Google)* for providing detailed, timely feedback on the initial drafts.

Thanks to Ritesh Reddy, Rishma Jivan and Kapil Kumar, the young managers, and potential great leaders of tomorrow for stepping in to summarise the book at very short notice.

Nirrbhay Raghavan, a Grade X student, who agreed without any hesitation to assist me with the initial transcripts, and Aditi Thirumannamalai, a Grade IX student, for the artwork she provided.

I am highly indebted to many saints, philosophers, and leaders of the world from both the past and the present times who inspired me with their invigorating leadership qualities and doctrines.

I am thankful to my father-in-law, Natesa Sitaraman, and mother-in-law Meena, for encouraging me in the spiritual path and leading me to my Guru Sri Sathya Sai Baba.

I am ever grateful to my mother Nagalakshmi, father G. Govindarajan, brother G. Jayaraman, and sister Jaya Balakrishnan. They have taught me good values and a positive attitude from childhood through inspiring stories from the great epics of Ramayana, Mahabharata, and the scriptural classic Srimad Bhagavatam. These values imbibed a positive attitude in me and provided encouragement throughout my career, coming in especially handy during the writing stage.

I am thankful to my sons Dhananjay Bharadwaj *(Senior Director, Navis)* and Prashant Bharadwaj *(Professor of Economics, UCSD)*, for their insightful inputs. My granddaughters Mridula and Meera who nudged me, from time to time, to complete the book sooner, so that I could be available to them and not be distracted with my book.

Without my wife Lalitha's support, I wonder how I could have finished this book. Her willingness to carry the extra responsibility of managing our home by herself while also dealing with the complexities caused by Covid-19 and the lockdown was challenging. I deeply admire her support.

Lastly, and most importantly, I am grateful to my God, guru, and guide, Sri Sathya Sai Baba, for kindling the fire in me to undertake this project and providing the divine direction from the stage of ideation to completion.

I offer my heartfelt gratitude to one and all with humility and respect.

November 4, 2021   *G. Jagannathan*

Author's Note

Heart and soul of leadership

I s this reality? Or is it a dream? I found myself under the blue skies where the sound of ocean waves breaking on the rocks was soothing to the soul. One could oversee the locked-in glittering golden patch of sand enclosed within the black stones on the far right and the sand dunes on the far left. I could see this from the oversized windows on the ninth floor.

FUTURE OF THE WORLD

Well, I was inside a room. It appears that I was a silent witness as a backbencher in a conference room where deliberations were underway among eleven top global leaders from different continents. Various fields were represented in the conference room to discuss the future of the world. The chairperson was a highly qualified judge. She was chosen by a unanimous vote.

Their single goal was to decide which type of leadership would lead the world to happiness, prosperity, and peace. They were struggling to select one unique quality that great leaders must have to achieve this goal. The panellists included a retired five-star general, a famous conductor of a philharmonic, a great painter, a famous cine actor, a well-known philanthropist, a successful CEO of a Fortune 500 company, a Nobel laureate, a renowned cardiac surgeon, a nerd from Silicon Valley, and a gold medalist from the last Olympics.

MENTAL BATTLES

They were engaged in their selection process but were unable to proceed towards a consensus. The painter got tired, stood up and said, *"Let's get some fresh sunlight,"* and he went to open the curtains. Through the well-polished and clean glass window, they could see the beautiful ocean waves, the glittering sand dunes, and the open blue sky outside. The general, who was next to the painter, saw some angels flying low. The general noticed that the angels were trying to attract the attention of the panellists. He immediately drew the attention of the others to this rare sight.

They all stepped into the beautiful lush green lawns in front of the building overlooking the vast ocean upon which the sun's rays danced as if to point to and reaffirm that the ocean was indeed a metaphor of abundance, if only one could open one's mind.

The wonder of wonders, the five angels, smilingly descended in front of the leaders.

Looking at the awestruck faces of the leaders, one of the angels spoke in a sweet voice:

"We are angels with extraordinary powers, and each of us can help you resolve your problems easily. Tell us if anything is bothering you?"

The philanthropist responded by explaining the purpose of their meeting, which was to decide one quality that every future leader should possess to ensure happiness, prosperity, and peace for all the beings on this planet. He said:

"The contest is very tough, and many were in the prelims, but only five qualified for the finals. Now is a great moment, and we are struggling to decide the winner."

The angel who seemed enthusiastic said,

"That is very interesting, and may I know who the finalists are?"

The Nobel laureate replied,

"We would be delighted to share if you promise to keep this a secret."

The angels gave the assurance, and he continued,

> *"The five finalists are Teamwork, Excellence, Respect, Humility, and Action. After several rounds of discussion, we concluded that all other traits are sub-sets of these five. We are equally divided on our choice of the single most important trait. Could you please help us resolve this?"*

The angels quickly glanced at each other and shared a broad smile. They talked amongst themselves for some time, and one of the angels spoke up:

> *"We will surely help. It is such a coincidence that each of us is the guardian angel of those qualities you mentioned. You require all the angels to help you to decide the winner. However, only one of us will come with you to the conference room. You select just one of us. Which guardian angel do you want to go with you? Teamwork, Excellence, Respect, Humility, or Action?"*

OMG NOT AGAIN

"OMG! Not again. Do we have to decide on which angel's help we need? Coming to a consensus is the problem," they thought. The panellists tried their best to decide, and it was challenging to arrive at a decision. The chairperson of the selection committee decided to have a chat with the five angels. She met them one by one separately. She learned that the angels did not like the idea of being together even to help the panellists as they had

different processes and models for assisting the selection committee to decide the winner, except one of them.

When she communicated this view to the selection committee members, the ten leaders asked in unison:

> *"Which guardian angel is the exception?" She said, "The guardian angel of Humility is the exception. Angels of Teamwork, Respect, Excellence, and Action wanted separate identification, whereas Humility was willing to step aside and allow others the first place!"*

There was complete silence in the room for some time, until one of the panel members spoke up.

> *"My choice is clear. I want the guardian angel of Humility to come and help us".*

The second leader said, *"I agree." And put up his hand.*

Soon, all others joined and voted in favour of the guardian angel of Humility.

They decided to call only the guardian angel of Humility to the conference room to help them decide. As the angel for Humility entered the room, the top ten leaders were surprised to see that the other four also entered the room following Humility. When asked, the angels replied, *"We are angels for Excellence, Action, Respect, and Teamwork. We follow Humility whenever and wherever Humility is predominant. It is automatic."*

THE REALISATION

The guardian angel of Excellence said:

> *"Humility is our leader that shows courage, willingness to learn irrespective of age and gender, better inter-personal relationships, and recognises people for their good actions and success rather than arrogating all credits to itself. I am always present where humility is exhibited."*

The angel of Action entered next and said, *"Excellence follows Humility and I cannot stay back. Actions speak volumes and convey more than what the leaders want to say, and it is Actions that reflect Excellence."*

Respect sneaked in next. The general was curious to know why the guardian angel of Respect was entering the room when it did not want to enter in the first place.

The angel of Respect said:

> *"Well, wherever Humility, Excellence, and Action are present, my presence is inevitable. The outcomes are very positive. Respect for people, time, nations, cultures, languages, and different faiths grow. All this is the direct result of Humility, Excellence, and Action coming together. Hence, I follow them"*

Finally, the angel for Teamwork entered and said:

"How can I stay back? My high performance and happiness solely depend on the fact that the credit for success remains with the Team and not the leader. Moreover, to be effective and efficient, I depend on the leader's Humility, Excellence, Action, and Respect. Hence, I could not stay outside but followed them, although not invited!"

I WOKE UP WITH A CLEAR HEAD

Indeed, dreams have the power to transmit from the subliminal to the elevated conscious mind. Over the years, I have reflected upon leadership as a subject. It has been a topic discussed for the longest time and continues to attract attention, even in the present times, and probably will continue to be discussed so long as humanity exists. Humans on Earth date back a few million years. Older civilisations that date back to a few thousand years have treasure troves of experiences and innate learnings. Many teachings from China, Egypt, Europe, Africa, and the Indian subcontinent have so much to offer. I will share what I imbibed from the rich message of the 7,000 years old philosophical scriptures and the legends from Indian epics. Qualities of a good leader are mentioned in the Ramayana and the Mahabharata, the two great and sacred epics from India that date back over 7,000 years. The point is that the epics are ancient and so is leadership.

LEARNING IS EVERYWHERE

The great Sage Valmiki, who wrote the Indian epic Ramayana, mentions dozens of qualities that a great emperor like Rama personified. The legend of Rama has been a perennial source of solace for millions of people over hundreds of centuries. The hundred percent perfect character of Rama has been exemplary, energising, and the everlasting essence of leadership. Another inspiring personality was Bhishma, the great-grandsire of the Pandavas and Kauravas, of the Kuru dynasty from the epic Mahabharata. In his conversation with King Yudhishtira, he elaborated on what a great king should and should not do, thus listing the qualities of a great ruler. This is documented in detail by Sage Veda Vyasa, around fifty centuries before Christ in the section titled 'Shanti Parva' of the epic Mahabharata. Chanakya, the great teacher, philosopher, royal advisor, economist, and political strategist during the Maurya Dynasty (around 4th Century BC), listed three qualities that defined a great leader. While Napoleon Bonaparte is said to have listed approximately eight dozen traits of a good leader, and the list goes on.

If one carefully analyses the multiple traits listed by different great people and researchers, one will notice they all fall into five groups. This book aims to focus on and discuss these. An attempt is made here to filter, select, and elaborate on just five traits: Humility, Excellence, Action, Respect, and Teamwork, which I call by the acronym, the HEART of Leadership.

Over the years, based on my personal experience, I place leaders into four levels. Selfish, Good, Great, and those who are Inspiring. Without the HEART, a leader, however powerful (s)he may be, remains at the lowest level, at the base, and are regarded as 'Selfish Leaders' from the point of view of the world. They may have brought benefits to a small group, or themselves, but were responsible for the overall destruction and suffering of millions of people. History is replete with examples of these dangerous leaders. They have waged world wars that have been fought at a phenomenal cost of human lives, property, and resources.

The next level is that of 'Good Leaders', those who show some traits of HEART and give results that generally benefit many in the organisations they serve and a few from outside. Generally, history does not record their names as they are normal and not out of the ordinary. Then we come to the level of 'Great Leaders' who show extraordinary qualities of HEART. They are in small numbers, and they work sincerely for the wellbeing of people across the organisation they serve, the community at large, and for the environment. They usually play win-win. They are the ones who are listed in the Top 100 of reputed magazines and industry associations. These are fundamental qualities that every aspiring leader should develop.

These five qualities derive strength and energy from a super causal quality, the Soul of the leader. When HEART is combined with the Soul, they become legendary and are chosen as the 'Inspiring Leaders' of the Millenia. They can be counted on fingertips. Inspiring Leaders are one of a kind, suffused with

Love and Awareness. They are conscious of themselves, of others, and the whole universe at the same time. They have energy levels that are incredibly high. Humility, Excellence, Action, Respect, and Teamwork are part of their DNA. It is their second nature and comes to them naturally. I have reflected on these aspects in detail in Chapter 6 titled 'It Is Deep Within'.

A BOOK WITH A DIFFERENCE

This is not an autobiography. This book is a compilation of my reflections based on the experience of over 40 years and my work that has put me in touch with over 42 nationalities across 57 countries. I had the good fortune of being touched by Inspiring Leaders from very close proximity. They shaped my outlook on life in many ways.

In this age of digital and remote working, many young aspiring leaders will be poorer and impoverished by missing out on the richness of experiences. How can we transmit this wealth of experiences and reflections so it will sprout wings for budding leaders?

It all started a little more than a year back when Raghu Kalé, my friend, colleague, and CEO of Striking Ideas, and I were chatting about our 'good old days' of having worked with several leaders, many of them being common to both of us. We enjoyed recalling so many comfortable and not so comfortable instances of our interactions with these leaders. Soon the leaders list expanded and included many world leaders, across the continents, and from varied fields. Our observations and experiences were interesting. I started writing down the anecdotes, stories, and what I learnt from them. When I shared a few of them with my wife, Lalitha, she was surprised. She said, *"It is so interesting. How do you recollect these stories and incidents so vividly? You should write a book on Leadership based on your actual experience."*

During my conversation with Raghu, I proposed the idea of a book very hesitantly. Surprisingly, Raghu readily agreed, and he was ready with all the resources and a unique methodology to shape the narrative of this book, as he had set up a publishing wing in the new company he had incorporated. His involvement was consistent over an entire year with scheduled fixed-time meetings for monitoring progress. It is divine intervention when some paths get charted without much ado.

There were many distractions — lockdown conditions under Covid-19, anxiety about proper vaccines, delta variant, presidential elections in the USA, social media giving mixed and most often contrary news, and many more. However, with a clear focus, disciplined approach, monitoring progress, and partnering with God, it was possible to complete this effort.

The book has six chapters. Each chapter is devoted to one trait or quality of great leaders. The order of the chapters follows the acronym HEART – Humility, Excellence, Action, Respect, and Teamwork. Each chapter is complete in itself. It includes several examples from my own corporate and personal life and learnings from them that helped me succeed in my career. I have tried my best to be as accurate as possible since some experiences are more than four to five decades old.

I have included a *'Takeaways'* section and some pointed questions under the title *'Reflections'* at the end of each chapter.

The sixth chapter is exclusively on the Soul of the HEART leader and how it is directly related to leaders' awareness levels. The idea expressed here may sound philosophical, but it is very practical and all Inspiring Leaders, the highest level of leaders, in my opinion, exhibit this trait in abundance.

WHY THIS BOOK

I feel blessed to have had the fortune of working closely with at least 42 nationalities when I worked in a conglomerate revered for its good governance practices. My work brought me in close touch with inspiring leaders. I paid particular attention to great leaders that the world is in awe of, their strides and changing the trajectory of human progress. After 40 years of a fruitful working life, I have often reflected on how the digital age and the pandemic is stealing away an opportunity for young aspiring leaders to experience life with a deeply personal touch. This has bothered me. In this social media age, likes, pokes, and posts are a new genre. And I know that this New Age will provide new patterns of behaviour, and aspiring leaders will adapt. Despite my optimism, I thought it was time to pen all of the assimilated reflections I had gathered on inspiring leaders by writing a book *Reflections on Leadership — My Life Experiences*.

How Can You Benefit from this Book?

One of the young leaders who read the initial draft asked me, *"What is the best way to read this book and benefit?"*

The whole book can be read in one go within three hours! However, my recommendation is to read chapter by chapter in the order it is presented. At the end of each chapter, dwell on the 'Takeaways' and add a few more from your side. Reflect upon the questions listed and search your heart for an honest answer. This will help you in assimilating the learnings from the chapter. Continue reading and finish the book in about a week.

The book is written with young adults and current leaders in mind. The future of the world is in the hands of young adults and how they will lead others. Current leaders, who are in a position of power and influence could also benefit immensely. By imbibing the HEART and Soul of leadership, they can bring happiness, peace, and prosperity to all beings in the world.

In Conclusion

In discussing leadership, often lessons from the military are used to inspire business practices. I have devoted my life, backed by my 40 years in improving business directed towards serving human progress in many ways. Our strides in elevating humanity to a better world of tomorrow will need leading voices from the world of business, the elected leaders, and academia — as selfless leaders devoted to making a difference can infuse insights for future generations.

Around the world, the electoral base appears to be growing disproportionately with those who are opaque to reasoning and critical thinking. The global corruption perceptions index 2020 published by Transparency International shows a global average of 43%, where 100% would be a score that reflects very clean and 0% is highly corrupt — this, to my mind, is a surrogate symptom of failing leadership. The business world, too, has its perils that regulators face in enforcing governance standards. These are some alarming trends.

I am in no disillusion — and I know that it will take far more than my book to reverse these mega-trends, yet I know my book is one drop in this ocean of sanity and purity for those who can lead and make a difference.

I recognise that every leader can serve and inspire future generations — as a leader I believe one can reflect on the propositions in my book to be a voice of reason for aspiring leaders and help set a context in leadership. Self-help is the best help one can find to strengthen one's resolve.

This book is a compilation of Reflections that young aspiring leaders can read and absorb to help find an elevated path to enhance progress for humanity.

I am positive that the change will happen and will happen soon.

Enjoy reading!

*I have three precious things which I
hold fast and prize.*

*The first is gentleness;
the second is frugality;
the third is Humility,
which keeps me from
putting myself before others.*

*Be gentle, and you can be bold;
be frugal,
and you can be liberal;
avoid putting yourself
before others,
and you can become
a leader among men.*

— Lao Tzu

*Pride is concerned with
who is right.*

*Humility is concerned with
what is right.*

— Ezra Taft Benson

1. THE BEST KEPT SECRET

Humility is the secret ingredient that makes leaders great

T he Sun that we know, the star of the solar system we live in, is 864,400 miles in diameter. This is about 109 times the diameter of Earth. The Sun weighs about 333,000 times as much as our Earth. It is so large that about 1,300,000 Earths could fit inside. It turns out that our Sun is an average-sized star. There are much bigger stars than the Sun, some as big as 100 times the diameter of our Sun. The Universe has an estimated 350 billion large galaxies (like the Milky Way). It houses about 30 sextillion stars; that is 30,000,000,000,000,000,000,000 stars! The Earth is about 3.5 million times larger than a human. The Solar System is about 36 billion times larger than the Earth (3.6×10^{10}). [1a]

Humans are so infinitesimal when compared to this wonderful and vast universe. Just a speck of dust.

HUMILITY – THE DRIVER OF SUCCESS

My brother-in-law, Shiv Kumar, is one up when it comes to information updates. He has the art of picking up the current news from authentic sources and announcing the breaking news, better than the well-known media can handle. He is an engineer with a Master's in Chemical Technology and a Program on Global

Leadership diploma from Harvard. He had been a sales professional at a very senior level for a global company and achieved great success. The first time I heard about Jeffery Weiner was through Shiv when he broke the news about a new social media platform called LinkedIn, founded in 2002, that was connecting professionals of all industries across the world. That set my mind to read more about Jeffery, and I had even set up a Google Alert on news items related to him. In the last two decades, we have learnt so much about Jeffery Weiner, the current Executive Chairman of LinkedIn. As the CEO of LinkedIn, he created history by selling the company to Microsoft for a whopping US$ 26.2 billion in 2016.

Weiner graduated in Economics from the Wharton School at the University of Pennsylvania in 1992. His super performance as Vice President of Warner Bros., EVP at Yahoo, and Executive-in-Residence for venture capital firms like Accel Partners and Greylock Partners helped him rise at rocket speed in his professional career.

Prior to becoming the Executive Chairman of LinkedIn in June 2020, Jeff was the CEO of LinkedIn. During his 11 years at the helm, numbers on all fronts were soaring high in a positive direction.

One of the highlights of his leadership at LinkedIn was when he took the unprecedented step of donating $14 million stock bonus to employees in 2016 when the stock prices dropped. This decision convinced me that he was a philanthropist with a difference. His actions are a clear signal of his loyalty and affection to his employees. Indeed, a small token of appreciation — has more than what the eyes can see. Taking a line from the book by Raghu Kalé *'Loyalty and Sacrifice'*:

"Relationship's blossom when one enhances the value of the other without directly demanding a quid pro quo. The only way a relationship will last is if you are inclined to give more than you are willing to take." [1b] In this book, Raghu explains the fundamental principles and factors that drive loyalty. It is no secret that the praise for LinkedIn's culture is something that differentiates the company, as they actually care. [1c]

I wanted to know more about Jeffery and his approach to true success. Although, I've never had the privilege of meeting him in person, I've got to know his Mantra for success through an interview Scott Mautz conducted with Weiner. Scott wrote:

"When I asked Weiner the keys to his momentous success, he immediately said, 'You surround yourself with people a lot smarter than you, then empower them.' He later continued, 'Too many people die with their mistakes. When you make a mistake, admit it, correct it, and move on.'"

"He went on to say in response to how he manages a crazy portfolio of work, 'You can't do it all yourself. You have to entrust others.'"

'Humble leaders know they aren't the centre of the universe. Research also shows that humble leaders know the world doesn't revolve around them and are energised by this understanding.'

"Again, Weiner typified this finding. When I asked about his leadership philosophy, he said, 'It starts and ends with--it's not all about you. Humble leaders habitually empower and celebrate others. Humble leaders are willing to admit when they're wrong and accept help.'" [1d]

The ancient Indian scriptures have stressed and reiterated the importance of 'Satsang', the association with people of impeccable character. Surrounding oneself with a bad company of people could result in disastrous situations. This includes 'Yes-Men' who out of their own selfish interest keep saying 'Yes' to their boss' prattle and leads her/him to certain downfall.

EARLY LESSONS

As I was growing up in India, the one story I heard from my parents, very often from the Ramayana, the great Indian epic, was from one of its seven cantos titled 'Sundara Kand' meaning 'The Beautiful Canto'. The hero of this canto is Hanuman, the monkey who jumped across the ocean in search of Sita, the abducted consort of the exiled crown prince Rama. Hanuman is described as most courageous, brilliant, astute, and knowledgeable in all arts and sciences. He accomplished several tasks which could not be performed by even the most intelligent and skilled human beings and demigods. Yet he remained humble as a devotee of Rama, whom he considered as His Divine Master. Hanuman's humility is par excellence. This outstanding quality stuck in my mind from that early age. It made me wonder how someone could be so humble despite such accomplishments in life. Why is humility such a crucial leadership trait that people always end up praising and following those who demonstrate this quality?

Arrogance Bows Down Before Humility

In my school days, I read the story The Three Hermits by Leo Tolstoy. The original story was written in Russian sometime towards the end of the 19th century and translated into English much later. The story is about an arrogant bishop who meets three hermits living on an island while sailing on a ship between Archangel and the Solovetsky Monastery. On meeting the simple and illiterate hermits, the bishop enquires about their spiritual practice. With arrogance, the bishop informs them that he knows a better way to please God. With great difficulty, the hermits learn the new way to render the prayer. The bishop is finally satisfied that the hermits are now better prepared to offer service to God. He returns to the ship and continues his travel.

As the bishop sat and watched the colours of the sky change at dusk, he saw a light approaching him across the sea. It was an incredible sight as he saw the three hermits running on water towards the ship. The three hermits approached the bishop and told him that they had forgotten the prayer taught by him. They requested more lessons in prayer.

The bishop's arrogance was shattered. He was completely humbled by seeing the miracle of the hermits walking over the sea. He bowed to them and said, *"Please continue with your own prayer. That is sufficient to reach God. It is not for me to teach you. Pray for us sinners."* [1e]

The parable can be interpreted in so many ways, but I feel at its core is the humility of the three hermits that shines through.

THE GREATEST COMMON FACTOR

A glance at the leadership profile of highly respected leaders reveals that humility has been a unique and common characteristic of all great leaders, across the world. I am not referring to those who are in positions of power alone but in positions of influence as well. Such great leaders have a special place in the hearts of all people and are a class higher than other leaders.

Humility calls for courage, accepting ignorance, and a willingness to say, *"I don't know"*, or *"I admit I made a mistake"*, or *"I apologise for the wrongs I have committed"*. Such leaders have the simplicity to seek guidance and an earnest interest in continuous learning. In the four decades of my corporate life, I have worked with many leaders who displayed these characteristics very naturally.

Humility seemed to be their second nature. Some of my colleagues misunderstood the quality of humility as a sign of weakness. This perception is entirely wrong. Humility is the result of several factors such as a willingness to learn, good understanding, and high self-confidence. My experience confirms that whenever a person operates with the courage of conviction and adheres to truth and righteousness, humility expresses itself naturally.

When I think about my favourite leaders, they have been genuine and transparent. Mahatma Gandhi's autobiography *'My Experiments With Truth'* is classic proof of transparency to the core. Humble leaders have lived true to themselves with full faith in what they believed. Humility came to them as a natural by-product.

I have also come across many persons in positions of authority who worked for themselves and believed in taking full credit for their success and achievements. *"I did that", "I was the architect behind that success", or "It is my idea",* were words that came to them first. Other colleagues and the organisations they served came far behind! I believe that leaders who consistently make decisions to benefit their own self-interest leave unhealthy feelings and in the long run fail and are mostly forgotten or remembered for wrong actions.

It is simple logic to state that: *Humility is inversely proportional to ego-centric actions.*

Humility is directly proportional to one's courage to admit and say, *"I don't know."* It is directly proportional to the level of spiritual maturity. We will explore Humility vis-a-vis Spirituality later in the book.

A Deep Dive

Gen. James L. Anderson, USA (Ret.), and Dave Anderson in their seminal book *'Becoming a Leader of Character'*, write that to be a leader who exercises humility, one needs to believe and act in a way that genuinely demonstrates that we aren't full of ourselves.

Are we willing to say?

> *"I blew it. It's my fault."*
>
> *"I need some help."*
>
> *"I am listening."*
>
> *"I am keen to learn."*
>
> *"I have room to grow. "* [1f]

To become our natural way of expression, humility calls for a lot of practice. One must choose to be humble because pride and arrogance, such as, *"I am the Doer"*, *"It is My idea"*, comes naturally as a default response for most of us. This response is because of the messages that have been imprinted in our brain right from childhood by way of pampering our ego even for little things that we probably do not deserve.

A look at the nature around us will clearly demonstrate that the creator set up the whole universe in perfect condition and did not leave his signature behind for anyone to know!

In Vedanta, the most ancient Indian philosophy, it is pointed out that the whole universe is born, exists, sustained, and dissolves in pure consciousness, which we call 'God'. The purpose of life is to experience the divinity that exists in every being.

The Self-Realisation process results in what is commonly known as Nirvana, Moksha, Liberation, Absolute Freedom, and many more. In essence, it only requires fully dropping our ego. When we drop our ego, divinity manifests almost instantaneously.

The author C. S. Lewis, put it perfectly when he described Humility:

"If anyone would like to acquire humility, I can, I think, tell him the first step. The first step is to realise that one is proud. And a biggish step, too. At least, nothing whatever can be done before it. If you think you are not conceited, it means you are very conceited indeed." [19]

CANCELLING A BREAKFAST MEETING WITH THE US PRESIDENT

Here is a true story that I came across about Sam Rayburn, a congressman who served in the House of Representatives of the United States for almost seventeen years and wielded enormous political power. The story attracted my attention as it revealed to me the character of the person and how he demonstrated humility through his actions.

One day, Sam had an appointment with the President of the United States over breakfast. But when he learned that the teenage daughter of a friend had died in a tragic accident, he cancelled it by calling the President. He told the President that his friend was in trouble and therefore he could not come. Instead, he went to his friend's house to personally convey his condolences to the bereaved family. Sam asked his friend whether he needed any help. His friend replied that there was no need as all arrangements were already made. During the conversation, Sam learnt that his friend had not even had a cup of coffee since morning as he was very busy making all the arrangements for the funeral. Sam decided to make coffee for his friend! [1h]

Is Humility an innate quality?

When I was discussing great Leadership and its relationship with humility with young adult volunteers of a service organisation, one question stood out significantly. Is it possible to develop humility, or is it some inborn quality of great leaders? If the latter were the case, then this book or other self-development books would become meaningless, and we would need to sit and pray for humility to be bestowed upon us by God!

It is always good to be born with this trait. What if we are not but want to learn to be humble? One must make a conscious choice to exercise humility until it becomes a habit. Over time, our choice to act with humility will become our natural character.

But until humility becomes part of our DNA, we must make daily choices to exercise it at every opportunity that comes our way.

"Humility, as with all the habits of character, is like a muscle. You have to exercise humility to build humility," writes Dave Anderson. [1g]

Like regular exercise helps in building muscles, so also can we develop humility through constant practice? We should be aware that we need to practice.

After repeatedly studying the Indian epics, Ramayana and Mahabharata, observing the practices of great leaders, and reflecting on the lessons I learnt through my life experiences, I have come up with seven suggestions for developing Humility in our lives.

One — Observe More And Speak Less: Our human body has been engineered most efficiently by the Creator. He gave us two eyes to see, two ears to hear, two nostrils to breathe, two hands and two legs to work and walk. But He provided only one tongue to taste and speak! It means we are expected to learn more by observing, hearing, and working than speaking.

The less we speak about ourselves, the better it is. Remember the adage, *'speech is silver, silence is gold!'*

Two — Extend Basic Courtesies: The year 1974 introduced me to some of the legendary leaders from the Tata Group, and the most respected industrial conglomerate in India.

The Tata Group story is an unstoppable journey of India's most illustrious and inspiring business house that began in 1868 when a young Jamsetji Nusserwanji Tata set up a small trading company in erstwhile Bombay.

Today, the Tata Group comprises 30 companies across 10 verticals, with 750,000 associates spread over 100 countries across six continents. The group's revenue is over US$ 120 billion! The fascinating story of the Tatas from 1868 to 2021 introduces us to the legends who have kept the Tata flag flying high for more than 150 years and I just heard the breaking news that Air India is back into the Tata Group.

I joined the Tata Group's Commercial Vehicle Manufacturing company in Mumbai, India and my office was located across the street from Bombay House, the headquarters of the Tata Group.

I was in my office and got a call from the Joint Managing Director's office that he wanted to see me. This was just four days after I joined the company! My mind started to visualise different scenarios.

One thing I realised was that our mind could think different things faster than the speed of light! With rising adrenaline, and not having time to wait for the elevator, I climbed down the stairs from the fourth floor, two steps at a time, dashed across the street, and entered Bombay House, to reach the Jt. MD's office on the second floor. Luck was on my side, I thought, as I saw the elevator open and a few people entering it. My dash continued, and I entered the elevator brushing aside another person ahead of me lest I miss the elevator. When I turned to see the gentleman whom I had overstepped, I was in for a shock. It was none other than Jehangir Ratanji Dadabhoy Tata *(fondly called JRD).*

Before I proceed with my story, let me briefly introduce you to one of the most respected industrialists of India – JRD Tata. He was the legendary chairman of the Tata group of companies from 1938 to 1991. He took charge of the group at the young age of 33 and ran the group meticulously on the values of righteousness, integrity, and national interests for more than half a century.

Considered as the *'Father of Indian Aviation'*, JRD was the most respected industrialist and was conferred the Bharat Ratna (Jewel of India), India's highest civilian award in 1992. He remains the only businessman in India to have received this honour.

Back to our story. I immediately stepped out of the elevator and said, *"I am sorry, Sir, it is my mistake".* JRD simply smiled and said, *"That's alright young man, you are in a hurry, please go ahead. I can wait."* I was so ashamed that I had the courage neither to face him nor to turn and look at the others in the elevator. I learnt my lesson the hard way! I also learnt that it takes a lot more effort to crack the ego of human beings, or to put it another way, to break the 'youthful exuberance' like I had at that time.

JRD was exemplary in his courtesies that instantly brought his humility to the forefront.

Later, with sincere and deliberate effort, I started consciously practising simple courtesies and extending them to one and all. Soon it became my habit. In 1974, I was transferred to Jamshedpur.

This beautiful industrial town is named after the founder of the Tata Group, Jamsetji Nusserwanji Tata. He initiated the first steel plant in the country here, Tata Iron and Steel Company, now called Tata Steel. The steel plant came up first, way back in the early 1900s. Today, the city hosts hundreds of large, medium, and small industries contributing to more than US$ 25 billion in sales. A big credit for spurring socio-economic development in this very underdeveloped region goes to the Tata companies.

I remember clearly how one of my early bosses used to greet people. It was my habit to wish my colleagues, *"Good morning, how are you doing today?"* when I met them in the office on arrival. This greeting coming genuinely from the heart and not mechanically uttered set the right mood for a productive day. Almost all of them felt happy, smiled, and responded positively except this particular boss. He used to respond by saying *"morning"* in a sheepish way! He was not in the habit of adding a *'good'* to the morning wish! It is just a courtesy, and one does not lose anything. Probably he had not learnt the costly lesson as I had a few years earlier with the Group Chairman!

Three — Accept Mistakes Openly: A very powerful tool to win friendship, confidence, and overcoming future discomfort is to say, *"I am sorry, I made a mistake".* It is so powerful that it can unnerve even our enemies.

I had the privilege of working for one of the best-run steel plants in India, Tata Steel. During my years with the company, the Managing Director, Russi Mody (1974-1993) had initiated a dialogue session with all senior executives, once every two months, to update the executives on the company's performance as well as to seek ideas and suggestions from them on company-related matters. This forum provided much-needed two-way communication between senior executives and the top management. It also helped build camaraderie among the attendees in a friendly way. This session was popularly known as *'Senior Dialogue'*. Dr. Jamshed J Irani, after taking over as Managing Director from Russi Mody in 1993, continued the tradition with great success. It was like a town hall meeting exclusively for 200 senior leaders from various divisions.

In the late 1980s, Tata Steel faced a serious problem with productivity and the cost of steel production. This became even more relevant in the global scenario as the need to become competitive after the Indian economy opened up to international competitors in the early 1990s was an existential requirement.

The company had set a very ambitious vision of *'becoming the lowest cost steel producer in the world'* sometime in 1996-97. This vision had been achieved by 1999-2000, and the new vision was yet to be decided. At that time, I was the Chief of Total Quality and Reengineering Division of the company, and I thought I should point out this lapse to the top management. Actually, it was my ego, *'I have found something the management has not been focusing on, and I must show my brilliance to all my colleagues!'* I rationalised it by telling myself that it was my duty. So, prompted by my ego, in one of the Senior Dialogues, which was usually held in the morning hours, I raised the point and drew the attention of the MD, that it was time the company should revisit its vision. I thought it was logical and a good reminder to the leadership team. The MD replied curtly, *"That's not your concern,"* and literally shut me up. I was dumbfounded. My ego was directly attacked. I felt numb, extremely low and shattered. After the meeting, a few of my colleagues gave me a sympathetic look, but rather, stayed away from me!

The same day, sometime in the late afternoon, I happened to meet Dr. Irani in the hallway of the main office building. He was about to walk down the staircase, along with two of his Deputy MDs, when he noticed me. He stopped me and said: *"Jaggu, I am sorry for having been rough with you this morning in the Senior Dialogue. I am going to Jaipur with my strategy team and during the next three days we will discuss our new vision and take it forward."* I was touched by his words and said, *"I am extremely sorry, Sir, that I raised this point in the Dialogue this morning. I realise my mistake."* Dr. Irani said, *"That's alright. It was a good reminder."* All my morning sorrow flew away! In those few words, Dr. Irani, the MD of India's largest steel company, clearly showed his humility and his bias for action. He was a great boss to work for.

I learnt my lessons. Firstly, never act prompted by ego. Secondly, if I had an idea or a suggestion, it should be discussed in a private setting rather than in a larger forum. The idea is not to win public attention but to get your suggestion or thought accepted and acted upon appropriately. Lastly, if I make a mistake, then I should, without any hesitation, admit it and seek apologies.

My learnings resonate with the research of Bradley Owens and David Hekman on humble leadership. Through interviews with leaders from the military to manufacturing to ministry, field research and lab experiments, they concluded that the hallmark of a humble leader is her/his willingness to admit mistakes and limitations. [1i]

Four — Accept Criticism With A Smile: Even though I recovered from the shock of ego-bruising, I went in search of literature on how to overcome criticisms, entertaining different perspectives at the same time, and respecting others irrespective of their views. I was studying various books written by my Guru, Sri Sathya Sai Baba, a revered spiritual master from India. I came across a piece of his writing on criticism that gives a different perspective. He says that one should be thankful to the person for his criticism, as he allows us to introspect honestly and dispassionately. If the criticism is valid, then we have a chance to correct and lead a better life. If the criticism is not true, then one may ignore and still feel thankful to the critic for presenting a different point of view. Since reading this and practising it, I have gained a lot in life.

Both ways we gain. Where is the need to feel upset? Wear a smile always. Follow the simple ABC of life – Always Be Cheerful.

Five — Love All Serve All, Help Ever Hurt Never: Sri Sathya Sai Baba summarised the entire ancient Indian scriptures in two maxims with just eight words – 'Love All Serve All, Help Ever Hurt Never.' Each maxim is so powerful. This stems from the Vedantic Truth that God resides in every being and serving the needy is akin to serving God. Mother Teresa, the catholic nun from India who was canonized as Saint Teresa of Kolkata in September 2016, lived this basic principle in her life by serving the homeless, sick, and the poor in Kolkata, India, as she saw Jesus in every human being. Serving others helps the person who serves more than the person served! To enable spiritual seekers to practise his maxims, Sri Sathya Sai Baba created a service organisation in 1965. The mission was to help volunteers from all over the world, irrespective of caste, colour, race, power, position, wealth, gender, and geographic differences to serve the needy and alleviate human suffering with humility. Fifty years later, nearly a million volunteers from across 125 countries continue to use the platform for their personal transformations, and for contributing to societal wellbeing.

Let's look at another continent for diamonds of character. For diamonds where could anyone go but Africa! The most lustrous diamond of Africa is the Nobel Peace Prize winner – Nelson Mandela. He underwent incarceration for several decades because he fought against apartheid. In the evening of his life, he gained moral victory and became the First President of an egalitarian South Africa in May 1994. Helping people in trouble and never wanting to hurt someone's feelings came to him naturally. Jessie Duarte, who was Nelson Mandela's assistant between 1990-94 recollects this story of his boss, which clearly demonstrates his attitude of never wanting to hurt anyone's feelings.

> *"He always made his bed, no matter where we travelled. I remember we were in Shanghai, in a very fancy hotel, and the Chinese hospitality requires that the person who cleans your room and provides you with your food, does exactly that. If you, do it for yourself, it could even be regarded as an insult.*
>
> *So, in Shanghai, I tried to say to him, 'Please don't make your bed, because there's this custom here.' And he said, 'Call them, bring them to me.'*

So, I did. I asked the hotel manager to bring the ladies who would be cleaning the room, so that he could explain why he has to make his bed, and that they do not feel insulted. He didn't ever want to hurt people's feelings. He never really cared about what great big people think of him, but he did care about what small people thought of him."

Another close associate of Nelson Mandela was South African photographer, Steve Bloom, whose father Harry Bloom was a political activist, and narrates this anecdote:

"During the 1950s my parents, who were anti-apartheid activists, knew Nelson Mandela. I remember the story he told them about the occasion he saw a white woman standing next to her broken car in Johannesburg. He approached her and offered to help. After fiddling with the engine, he fixed the car. Thankful for his help, she offered to pay him six pence.

'Oh no, that's not necessary,' he said, 'I am only too happy to help.' 'But why else would you, a black man, have done that if you did not want money?' she asked quizzically. 'Because you were stranded at the side of the road,' he replied." [1j]

Another presidential gem is Dr. A P J Abdul Kalam, who was sworn in as the eleventh President of India in July 2002. No other President of India has won the hearts of its citizens as unanimously as he did during his five-year term. He was fondly called 'The People's President.' He was a visionary, scientist, educator, music lover, and best known for his impeccable character. Every chapter of this book could feature him, but here I will focus on his humility.

I have heard him as the keynote speaker at one of the Quality Summits organised by the Confederation of Indian Industry (CII) in Bengaluru. As a scientist, his contribution to building India's civilian space power, and military missile development efforts using indigenous resources, is noteworthy. He was very humble about his achievements and came off as a smiling, friendly person, and very easy to mingle with. The Government of India had conferred on him the Bharat Ratna, India's highest civilian award in 1997. For all his achievements, his humility was outstanding!

Here is an incident that was shared by my colleague S. A. Vaneswaran, the first CEO of Tata Quality Management Services, who had the privilege of working with Dr. Kalam as a scientist in the Defense Research and Development Organization from 1982 to 1989. This illustrates the simplicity, humility, responsibility, and genuine concern for others by Dr. Kalam and Field Marshal Sam Manekshaw. Sam was the first five-star General of the Indian Army to be honoured with the title of Field Marshal by the Government of India. He was known for his strategic thinking, high discipline, quick wit, and care for his soldiers. He led his forces from the front.

"Dr. Abdul Kalam, as the President of India, was visiting Coonoor, in the Nilgiri Hills of South India. On reaching the place, he came to know that Sam was in the Military Hospital, in Wellington, close by. Dr. Kalam wanted to make an unscheduled visit to Sam. Arrangements were quickly made. At his bedside, Dr. Kalam spent about fifteen minutes talking to Sam and enquiring about his health.

Just before leaving, Dr. Kalam asked Sam, 'Are you comfortable? Is there anything I could do? Do you have any grievance or any requirement that would make you more comfortable?' As the President of India, Dr.Kalam was the Supreme Commander of the Defense Forces.

Sam said, 'Yes. Your Excellency, I have one grievance.' Shocked with concern, Dr. Kalam asked him what it was. Sam replied, 'Sir, my grievance is that I am not able to get up and salute my most respected President of my beloved country.' Dr. Kalam held Sam's hand as both were in tears.

Sam also told President Dr. Kalam that he had not been paid the pension as the Field Marshall for nearly twenty years. An aghast President Dr.Kalam went to Delhi and sanctioned the pension with arrears within a week and sent the cheque of nearly Rs 1.25 crores (approximately US$ 250,000 at that time) through the Defense Secretary by a special plane to Sam. When Sam received the cheque, he promptly donated it to the Army Relief Fund!" [1k]

My colleague SA Vaneswaran who shared this anecdote asked a poignant question, *"Whom will you salute now – Sam or Dr.Kalam!?"*

A tribute to President Dr. Kalam's humility came from President Barack Obama, through the office of his Press Secretary on the 28th July 2015, the day Dr. Kalam culminated his earthly sojourn.

"On behalf of the American people, I wish to extend my deepest condolences to the people of India on the passing of former

Indian President Dr. APJ Abdul Kalam. A scientist and statesman, Dr. Kalam rose from humble beginnings to become one of India's most accomplished leaders, earning esteem at home and abroad. An advocate for stronger US-India relations, Dr. Kalam worked to deepen our space cooperation, forging links with NASA during a 1962 visit to the United States. His tenure as India's 11th president witnessed unprecedented growth in US-India ties. Suitably named 'the People's President' Dr. Kalam's humility and dedication to public service served as an inspiration to millions of Indians and admirers around the world." [1l]

When I had gone to see Mr. S Chandrasekhar, Executive Director, Higgins Botham Books Publishers, India, the discussions turned to Dr. Kalam. He recalled his meeting with the President at the Rashtrapati Bhavan (The Presidential Residence) in the capital city of New Delhi.

"The President received me warmly and spoke to me in Tamil, my native language. He was concerned about students and youngsters and wanted to see that they get the best education. I could see the noble spirit of a teacher in him, speaking from the heart. He treated me as if I was at the same level as him and knew me for decades. His humility was evident throughout our meeting. Truly President Dr. Abdul Kalam was a great leader, very rare to find in the 21st century." [1m]

Six — Learning Is Supreme: Have you ever wondered how much we know? In the world of the Internet, we have access to the entire spectrum of knowledge. But do we have the attitude and aptitude for learning and the courage to say "I don't know" when we do not know something?

During my professional career, I took a great liking for Training and Development. As a trainer, I had an excellent opportunity to realise that learning does not depend on the position you hold or your age. There is a common misconception that training programmes are meant primarily for junior employees. The senior employees often nominate their juniors with the notion that training may not be necessary for their position in the organisation.

I was conducting a training programme on Excellence some years back in Singapore. One of the senior executives later met me and told me, *"You know what, I was very keen on attending your programme, but I forgot to note down the date and time of the programme in my calendar!"*

On the contrary, here is an example of JRD Tata, on what he thought of learning, irrespective of his age and position.

This was in the year 1990. I was heading the Value Engineering Division at Tata Steel. Every year the company used to celebrate Founder's Day, on the 3rd March the birthday of Jamsetji Tata. On this day, the company used to organise an exhibition of success stories and this exhibition was open to all in the company to attend and see for themselves the achievements of various divisions and departments over the years. As head of Value Engineering, I was asked to showcase how we had improved performance at a reduced cost. On the 3rd March, this was inaugurated, and the first visitors were the Board of Directors of Tata Steel. Incidentally, Tata Steel used to hold a Board Meeting on the same day at Jamshedpur.

Since VIPs were coming to see the exhibits, each department head was asked to represent his or her stall. I had the privilege of managing the booth on Value Engineering. Right after the inauguration, JRD, our Group Chairman, arrived. He was patiently going through various stalls and curiously observing and hearing the success stories. When he came to my booth, he was more than eager. An octogenarian by then, he was carefully scanning all the exhibits and listening to my narration with rapt attention. As it was time for the Board Meeting, Russi Mody, then MD of the company, reminded JRD that they had only five more minutes to go back to the Board Meeting. That was very disappointing news for me. I thought of having the privilege of an extended conversation with JRD and realised that the lifetime opportunity is going to last only for a couple of more minutes. But JRD surprised everyone. He looked at Mody and said, *"Russi, you know, I had learnt a little about Electrical Engineering, Metallurgical Engineering and Mechanical Engineering, but I had not heard about Value Engineering. This seems to be remarkably interesting and unique. I want to learn more from this young man here. Can I come a few minutes late for the meeting?"* JRD spent his next twenty minutes with me, questioning and deepening his appreciation for the subject. To date, he has been the most senior and valuable student in any of my programmes. What an attitude to learning and what humility!

Mahatma Gandhi, venerated in India as Father of the Nation said, *"Learn as if you were going to live forever. Live as if you were going to die tomorrow."* One of my grand uncles, R. Sankaran Iyer, who served Mahatma Gandhi at the Sevagram Ashram, near Wardha, India, told me that Gandhi used to find a half an hour time slot to learn Tamil language from him, every week, despite his otherwise extremely busy schedule. Alvin Toffler, the American writer, futurist, and businessman, known for his works discussing modern technologies, including the digital revolution and the communication revolution, said, *"The illiterates of the 21st century will not be those who cannot read and write, but those who cannot learn, unlearn, and relearn."* [1n]

Seven — Give and Forgive: The problem with most human beings is that we want help, compassion, love, and many other things from others but seldom reciprocate. We get and forget! *"Of course, not true,"* you may say. Yes, there are always exceptions. But here we are not discussing exceptions. It takes a lot more fortitude and courage to give and continue to give even if the receiver is ungrateful.

Mother Teresa faced a lot of challenges when she was helping the sick and abandoned people on the streets of Kolkata. Though she was helping the locals, many were opposed to the idea and assumed different motives behind the charity. But she stood strong, continued, and forgave those who opposed her. She was convinced about her work and continued to give and give more. She is the epitome of Selfless Service, Sacrifice, and Simplicity. Humility was in her DNA. She never sought out fame and awards. On the contrary, they chased her! Organisations felt honoured by bestowing awards on her. The Nobel Prize Committee did itself well by recognising

Mother Teresa with the Nobel Peace Prize in 1979. The government of India conferred on her the Bharat Ratna in 1980.

Here is a quote from Mother Teresa that has inspired me and perhaps many millions:

> *"Humility is the mother of all virtues - purity, charity, and obedience. It is in being humble that our love becomes real, devoted, and ardent. If you are humble nothing will touch you, neither praise nor disgrace, because you know what you are. If you are blamed, you will not be discouraged. If they call you a saint, you will not put yourself on a pedestal."*

RESEARCH ON HUMILITY

Before I continue with my stride on some great examples of world-famous personalities, I would like to discuss some of my own informal research findings on what we have discussed so far on Humility.

Right from my school days, I have seen without exception that outstanding students, all of whom were rank holders, were very simple and honest. They were humble and carried that humility with them and which prompted them to learn more and become better learners. I remember them, including their names, even today, after almost 50 years later, because they taught me lessons on humility. I do not shy away or feel discouraged when it comes to learning, be it from a scholar or an expert, irrespective of their age. During the Covid lockdown, my eight-year-old granddaughter Mridula taught me how to share screens and some tricks on the use of a whiteboard in a Zoom meeting! This has helped me to learn and quickly adapt myself to the new circumstances. It not only relieves stress but also improves productivity. I noticed this trait in the world-class leaders we discussed earlier in this section. Modern-day research corroborates my informal conclusions.

Leaders are more powerful when they are humble. Humility helps them to learn, understand the limitations, expand their connections, encourage colleagues, empower team members, and be of service to society, as per new research findings. Ashley Merryman, in his inimitable style, writes in the Washington Post:

> *"True humility, scientists have learned, is when someone has an accurate assessment of both his strengths and weaknesses, and he sees all this in the context of the larger whole. He's a part of something far greater than he. He knows he is not the centre of the universe. And he's both grounded and liberated by this knowledge. Recognising his abilities, he asks how he can contribute. Recognising his flaws, he asks how he can grow. Humility's benefits turn out to be surprisingly concrete ... It isn't empty false praise or inflated self-esteem or tearing others down that pushes us to work to become our best selves. It's humility."* [1p]

THE LADY WITH A SMILE

To be precise, 654 women across the world have achieved success and which many in the world fear to dream! An exceedingly rare distinction of climbing 29,028 feet, the tallest mountain peak in the world, Mount Everest. Bachendri Pal, from India, is one of those rare gems.

Bachendri Pal was the first Indian woman to climb Mount Everest, and the fifth woman in the world to do so. She won several national awards including the Arjuna Award in 1986, the Padma Shri in 1994, and the Padma Bhushan in 2019 from the Government of India.

I had the good fortune of knowing her as a colleague while working at Tata Steel. She was the Chief of Tata Steel Adventure Foundation. Despite all her world-class achievements, she was an amazingly simple person with high ideals.

I learnt from her a few lessons on humility, excellence, respect for people, bias for action, and most importantly on how to achieve peak performance as a member and leader of a team.

From humble beginnings to achieving world-class recognition had been a steep climb for Bachendri Pal. She completed her bachelor's degree in Education (B. Ed) from Dehradun, but then found herself at home as there were not many job opportunities. 'Luck favours the brave' goes the saying.

Encouraged by Col. Prem Chand, Vice-Principal of the Nehru Institute of Mountaineering, she set her eyes on climbing peaks, and as a natural-born adventurist, she chose to conquer the tallest peak in the world. She was soon selected to be part of the Everest expedition.

She climbed the formidable highest peak, Mount Everest, on the 23rd May 1984. Although she could not forever leave her footprints on the highest snowy peak, she etched her name permanently into history.

When I met her for the first time in Jamshedpur, I asked her how she felt to be on top of the world. She smiled and said with great humility, *"I was very happy."* I asked her, *"You must have met with several challenges while undertaking the Everest expedition. How did you overcome those challenges?"* She said, *"There were hundreds of challenges and they had to be tackled, one by one. Good understanding among team members is essential and helps in overcoming challenges. What is required is a steady focus on the goal and strong willpower to never give up. Team members' constant encouragement enthuses one to surmount obstacles and tackle them effectively."* Not even once did she mention to me that her success was due to her own efforts. That I think is humility!

I believe that great leaders follow simple guidelines. I would like to conclude this chapter by highlighting the most important words I found from an anonymous source and that capture the essence of humility:

The six most important words are,
"I am sorry, I made a mistake."

The five most important words are,
"You did a good job"

The four most important words are,
"What is your opinion?"

The three most important words are,
"If you please."

The two most important words are,
"Thank you."

The one most important word is,
"We."

The least important words are,
"Me" and "I"

TAKEAWAYS

1. The most common characteristic of all great leaders is humility.
2. Humility can be developed through self-awareness and by practising a few simple steps regularly, such as:
   i. Always be courteous.
   ii. Eager to learn.
   iii. Serving others.
   iv. Accepting mistakes and standing corrected.
   v. Giving and forgiving.
3. Humility is the gateway to Inspiring Leadership.

REFLECTIONS

1. How often do I pride myself on my success?
2. How keen have I been to learn from my assistant?
3. How does humility win over team members' support?
4. When was the last time I accepted my mistakes and apologised for them?

The will to win,
the desire to succeed,
the urge to reach
your full potential ...

... these are the keys
that will unlock the door
to personal excellence.

— Confucius

2. MAKING AN IMPACT

I saw excellence in thought, word, and action

It is a great pleasure to visit Pier 39 in downtown San Francisco, for tourists shopping for souvenirs, but also for Bay Area locals. On a bright sunny Sunday morning, my wife and I drove to the beautiful city and spent the day enjoying the chill breeze on our faces and browsing for little nothings in the colourful shops with attractive displays. My eyes caught a small table display that included an energising quote by Vincent Thomas Lombardi:

"Excellence can be attained if you,

Care more than others think is wise,

Risk more than others think is safe,

Dream more than others think is practical,

Expect more than others think is possible."

I readily bought the souvenir and started thinking about its message after arriving home. What a beautiful definition of Excellence!

The same year in March 2011, I was in England to address Tata Technologies' annual leadership meeting on Business Excellence. After my address, a gold medalist at the Seoul Olympics, Adrian Moorhouse, from the UK addressed the participants. He had won a gold medal in the 100 metres breaststroke swimming competition in 1988. A passionate and engaging presentation followed. His presentation focused on his strategy to win the gold medal. I thought he was a living example of Excellence in action. When I got the chance to converse with him after his inspiring presentation, I asked him what his understanding of Excellence was. He gave a classic definition. He said, *"Excellence to me is being better than the best."*

It meant that in the pursuit of Excellence, there is no finishing line. I recall an inspirational short story from my schoolteacher Mrs Ranganayaki Krishnan. She was the senior teacher at Saraswati Vidyalaya, my alma mater, where I studied from Grade I to Grade XI. She was an inspiration to me. At a time when married women in India hardly took to higher education, she had completed her Master's in English, and a special degree in Teaching from Nagpur University, after her marriage. As a schoolteacher in Saraswati Vidyalaya, one of the top schools in the city of Nagpur, she encouraged her students to excel in whatever they were interested in. For example, seeing my interest in dramatics, she gave me different character roles in the school plays. She used to tell me several stories about great actors of her days, how they learnt the art and excelled in it.

She had retired from teaching sometime around 1986, and I had gone to meet her in Nagpur, to pay my respects. Seeing me after so many years she was simply overjoyed. During the long conversation that followed, I told her about my job and how I was engaged with Tata Steel. I added that this was an excellent company to work for in India. She thought for a moment and in her characteristic style narrated a story in Tamil mixed with English. She said, *"Jaggu, you mentioned 'excellent company', but do you really know what is Excellence? I want to tell you a story."* Here is the story:

"A king had a dream that his kingdom had the best temple of Lord Ganesha (an elephant-headed deity, who removes all obstacles in life as per Indian scriptures) in the whole world. On hearing about this dream, his council of ministers advised the king that he should start work on the new temple without any delay. The king was very happy and immediately started the search for the best sculptor and soon located him. He summoned the sculptor and said, 'I want you to undertake this job and finish it in one month. You may engage any number of sculptors for this job. I want the best idol to be sculpted and installed in the sanctum sanctorum. Remember that the idol must be the best in the world. I will reward you with thousands of gold coins.'

The sculptor agreed and started in earnest. Days passed, and the temple was ready in all respects except the main idol of Lord Ganesha. The king was worried about the delay and made a personal visit to the site to find out the reason. The king saw a beautiful marble stone carving of Lord Ganesha ready but was placed on top of a stone platform, while the sculptor was busy carving another big marble rock for the second idol of Ganesha.

Surprised, the king asked the sculptor, 'Do you need two statues of the same idol for the main shrine? One is enough, and we should proceed with the installation of the idol in the main shrine.'

'Yes, my Lord,' said the sculptor, busy with his work, 'I know we need only one, but the first one developed a hairline crack at the last stage.'

The king examined the first idol but did not find any crack.

'Where is the crack?' he asked.

'There is a crack on the back of the idol,' said the sculptor still busy with his work.

'Oh, at the back,' said the king with great relief. 'No one is going to see it anyway.

The sculptor stopped his work, looked up at the king and with folded hands said, 'But I know it!'" [2a]

The desire to excel is not dependent on whether someone recognises the effort or appreciates it. It essentially stems from within. It is an attitude based on what we value most.

In my long journey in the corporate world, I came across several leaders who showed this trait in everything they did. I am delighted to share them here to illustrate the point.

It was a momentous day in my life, the 6th February 2002. I went to the Air India Building in Nariman Point, Mumbai to meet S. Ramadorai, CEO and Managing Director of Tata Consultancy

Services that today, is one of the top three IT companies in the world, with more than 500,000 employees spread across 46 countries, and an annual sales revenue exceeding US$ 23 billion. That was my first day, joining Tata Consultancy Services, as Executive Vice President and Global Head of Business Excellence. We had an appointment at 9:30 AM. As soon as I arrived at his office, his secretary said, *"Yes, Ram is already waiting for you."* I said thank you, knocked on the door, and went into the room. He greeted me very warmly with a smile and said, *"Come, come and sit down, Jaggu"* (this is how I am usually addressed), in an honest and straightforward style. He said, *"I am pleased that you have joined this great organisation, and I look forward to driving excellence with your help."*

I was humbled. Here is the CEO of a vast multinational corporation aiming to hit the global top 10 by 2010, and he is saying he is going to drive excellence with my help. So, I said, *"Thank you very much, Ram, for this great opportunity. I want to share some thoughts on what I plan to do in the first six months. Please, see whether this meets your expectations."* He said, *"Yes, I am looking forward to that. Do you have a presentation to show me?"* I said, *"Yes,"* and I opened my laptop. He responded, *"Okay you can place it on this table,"* and he moved his chair and accommodated me next to him, so both of us could see the screen. I started the presentation. It had been only 15 seconds after I began my talk when Ram took a tissue from his table and wiped the dust that was on the laptop screen. He didn't say a word! I felt ashamed. Here I was sharing with him what I planned to do for driving excellence in the organisation, and silently, yet very powerfully, Ram was showing me, what excellence meant to him, and what it means to Tata Consultancy Services.

Excellence starts with every small aspect of our day-to-day activity. If we do not pay attention to them, how can we pay attention to larger facets of business? That was the first lesson for me in excellence in Tata Consultancy Services.

FLASHBACK ABOUT 50 YEARS!

The year was 1974, and I was working for Tata Motors, India's leading commercial vehicle company. I was a development engineer in the Ancillary Development Department. It was a lovely job, which combined both technical and commercial aspects of product development; products and components required in the assembly of the company's main product line, commercial vehicles (*also known as trucks*). I remember, distinctly, it was a Friday evening, when my colleagues and I were busy winding up our day's work so that we had time for planning the weekend. We were busy with our work, when our boss, Percy Ghyara, Executive-in-charge of the Ancillary Development, rushed out of his room, saying, *"I will be back soon, the Chairman is calling me. Please wait till I come."* The Chairman, Sumant Moolgaokar, was one of the great leaders of the Tata Group, who steered Tata Motors to the number one position in the Indian automotive industry by bringing in new products, introducing new technologies in manufacturing, and setting up one of the best Engineering Research Centres in India. His vision of setting up the Ancillary Development Division way back in the 1960s to help, guide, and establish small scale industries to manufacture precision auto components in the immediate proximity of the two manufacturing plants, at Jamshedpur and Pune, was visionary and praiseworthy. His desire for going beyond the expectations of customers, and his eye for minute details of precision were legendary. Today, Tata Motors is a global company, with world-class brands like Jaguar, Land Rover, and Daewoo in its ambit.

After meeting the Chairman, our boss came back and immediately called one of my colleagues, Arun Polke, to his room. Arun rushed in and within a minute came out and called me, *"Jaggu, you are also wanted."* So, I went in, not knowing what this was all about. Percy looked at me and asked, *"Do you know what this is?"* Incidentally, I was the newest addition to the Division, only a few weeks old in the organisation and was still going through induction training. He showed me something that looked like a brown plastic knob. *"It looks like a gear knob,"* I said, *"Exactly, it is a gear knob, and the Chairman's attention has been drawn by it,"* he replied as he turned to Arun. *"Do you know why?"* he asked him. *"May I have a look at the knob?"* Arun asked. He took the knob, and he said, *"Yes, this was very recently developed and introduced on the Semi-Forward Cowl Model."* Percy replied, *"Yes. You are right, but why did it draw the attention of the Chairman, that is my question?"* Arun looked at it very seriously, and I asked, *"May I also have a look at it."* So, we both looked at the gear knob very carefully, with microscopic eyes. But we couldn't find anything wrong with the knob. *"That is the problem. You guys are development engineers, you developed this product, and you don't know what the problem is!"* Percy said. *"But there doesn't seem to be anything wrong with the knob,"* replied Arun. Percy then said, *"No,* look at the letter 'R' on the knob." The brown knob had white markings for the respective gear numbers and 'R' was for the reverse gear.

Now when he mentioned the letter 'R', and we looked at it again, we could make out that the impression was not very good. I said, *"Yeah, the impression is not well embossed."* He said, *"Exactly. The Chairman was on his way back from Pune this morning, and at Khandala (a small town between Pune and Mumbai) he stopped when he saw a few of the Tata trucks parked on the highway near the Dhabas (highway-side restaurants). The Chairman saw one of the trucks, and he noticed that the letter 'R' was not correctly embossed. That caught his attention, and he made a note in his diary. When he reached his office, he immediately called me and asked why the embossing wasn't right."*

MAJOR ATTENTION TO MINOR DETAILS

The result of this *'attention to detail'* was obvious. Our weekend was gone! Arun and I rushed to the manufacturer's plant in Dombivli, then a suburb of Mumbai, on Saturday morning, and studied the process, from start to finish. We identified the cause of the problem and made the manufacturer modify the process. We made sure that the next lot met all the quality specifications. When Percy saw the sample from the new lot, he was happy and got approval from Moolgaokar.

The most important lesson for me was not how we solved the problem but paying major attention to minor details. The

Chairman of the company had an eye for detail, and he could catch a minor error on a gear knob, which is a tiny part of a 12-ton truck, and which consists of more than 5,000 different components and sub-assemblies, in a truck parked by a highway restaurant! But his attention to detail was excellent. It is no surprise that Sumant Moolgaokar is respected even today, nearly three decades after his demise, for bringing high-quality consciousness across the Indian sub-continent.

The same idea is echoed by General Colin Powell in his autobiography *'My American Journey'*, which was #1 on the New York Times Bestseller list. Under Colin Powell's rules on page 613, he writes, *"check small things"* as rule no. 8.

READY WITH TOOL KIT AT 30,000 FEET ASL!

JRD Tata, Chairman of Tata Group for more than 50 years, was an embodiment of excellence. His attention to detail was exemplary. JRD, as we stated earlier, was considered the Father of the Indian Civil Aviation industry. His passion for flying earned him the first flying licence in India. He launched Tata Airlines in 1932, the first commercial airline in India. It was nationalised by the Government of India in 1953 and became Air India. In 2021, Air India is back in the Tata fold.

In August 2020, during one of the video calls with ex-employees of the Tata Group, Dr. Jamshed Irani (*former MD of Tata Steel*) shared an incident that illustrates the point:

> *"JRD was travelling on an Air India flight, before the nationalisation of the airline. He observed that the light*

indicator that shows whether the restroom is occupied or not was malfunctioning. JRD asked the airline staff to rectify the indicator lamp switch. When they pleaded helplessness, he got up, took out from his bag a small tool kit, and said, 'Let me handle it.' After ten minutes, he returned to his seat, fully satisfied that the task was accomplished!"

"A memorable excerpt from one of his numerous memos addressed to the Air India management illustrates how JRD was a stickler for perfection and would promptly note down and communicate even small points of improvement he believed the airline should implement, 'The tea served on board from Geneva is, without exaggeration, indistinguishable in colour from coffee ... I do not know whether the black colour of the tea is due to the quality used or due to excessive brewing. I suggest that the station manager at Geneva be asked to look into the matter.'" [2b]

Some may say that these are random anecdotes or instances of leaders that bring out their streaks of excellence. Does it not demonstrate a passion for excellence and perseverance to pursue their set objectives, and patience beyond limits to achieve what they endeavoured to accomplish?

I now wish to explore how such leaders drive excellence across all facets of business in the organisations they manage.

THE JEWEL

I had the privilege of being associated with Business Excellence for well over 20 years in various capacities beginning as the Corporate Quality Head of Tata Steel, the CEO of the Tata Quality Management Services, a Division of Tata Sons, and Executive Vice President and Global Head of Business Excellence of Tata Consultancy Services. In all of these roles, I learnt that it was the responsibility of the leadership to set the whole organisation on the wheels of excellence and keep moving ahead on a journey that has no finishing line.

JRD Tata the former Group Chairman firmly believed that:

> *"One must forever strive for excellence, or even perfection, in any task, however small, and never be satisfied with second best."* [2c]

Taking over the mantle from JRD, in 1991, Ratan Tata excelled in establishing a process for perpetuating systems view in excellence across the Tata group companies and elevated it to a world-class level. I want to share with you here a little about Ratan Tata. In Hindi, the word *'Ratan'* means a precious gemstone. Indeed, he is a gem, a leader par excellence, and a jewel among world leaders. As the Chairman of the $120 billion Tata Group, he has the rare distinction of having driven excellence in all facets of business, be it in the areas of Process Management, Customer Experiences, Strategy Development, Corporate Governance, or Human Resources Practices. Ratan Tata was the Chairman of Tata Sons, the holding company of the Tata Group, from 1991 till his retirement on the 28th December 2012.

It all started with gaining wider awareness about the assessment framework from the Honeywell Quality Value (HQV) Award that the Tata joint venture, Tata Honeywell, had gained exposure to in 1993. This was a propelling factor as Madhu Bhagwat, then CEO of Tata Honeywell, SA Vaneswaran, then Quality Assurance Head, and Raghu Kalé, then Communications Head, feasted on the suggestions by a high-profile bureaucrat from Department of Electronics, Government of India Joseph Satyaraju. Having learnt about HQV, and ready to bestow the ISO certification upon Tata Honeywell, the bureaucrat suggested that Tata Group should have its own Quality Value Award. The trio were the spark behind crafting the initial proposal to engage the Group Chairman's mind as he was also the Chairman of Tata Honeywell. It took a few strides, and Group Chairman Ratan Tata in August 1995, announced the JRD Quality Value Award. This was known as JRD QV Award.

The Award, named after JRD, was aimed at not only commemorating the name of JRD Tata, who strived for Excellence all his life, but also to recognise those Group companies that achieved world-class benchmark level business performance.

Great leaders know how to bring
and retain the best talent within their orbit.

The years from 1995 to 1997 saw many board members and CEOs from around the Tata Group get involved as apex group and core group members, with SA Vaneswaran and Raghu Kalé garnering many hearts and minds to propel the JRD Quality

Value Award process. The dedication from JK Setna, who took over as Chairman of Tata Honeywell, and Ratan Tata was commendable. I asked Raghu to describe these initial years, as he was the anchor in Bombay House, the Tata group headquarters, in these formative years.

"JRD Quality Value lived in spirit, and there was no entity. It was pure passion, perseverance, and personal involvement from Ratan Tata and JK Setna. They were demanding the best and they expected nothing less. All this on shoestring budgets. And we knew, we somehow knew we were working on something big, something path-breaking, something that was about to change our trajectory. The initial years were a rocky ride, but we learnt a lot ..."

A few years after the award process was established, there was a need for a resource group centrally to help coordinate the various processes and one was set up. The genesis for creating such a group rested in recognising that the drive for excellence had to go beyond an award. Early on, the Group Chairman and his proponents realised that passion for improvement was more important than winning the JRD Quality Value Award. In 1996, Tata Quality Management Services was created under Tata Services with SA Vaneswaran heading it up from Bengaluru, as he was QA head for Titan Industries (Tata Group's lifestyle goods company), and Raghu Kalé in Bombay House. Later, SB Limaye joined the resource group and was based in Pune and CH Murthy in Bengaluru. With its fledgling start under Tata Services, its impact and contribution to the group were huge.

Passion indeed brings teams from across geographies.

The passion and some heavy lifting continued in Bombay House, and the realisation that the Tata brand is somehow connected to a robust system brought Tata Sons to elevate Tata Quality Management Services from Tata Services to Tata Sons, the parent company of the Tata Group. By 1998, Tata Quality Management Services had a strategic role to perform. Linking the Tata Group brand to standards of excellence milestones, and the Tata Code of Conduct formed the building blocks to go beyond the award process and get every Tata board to commit to high standards of professional, personal, and ethical excellence. While the JRD Quality Value criteria were fashioned on the Malcolm Baldrige National Quality Award criteria, in 1998, the criteria were renamed as the Tata Business Excellence Model.

Jim Setna, Director of Tata Sons, Ratan Tata, Group Chairman, and several Board Members, CEOs and high calibre executives were part of the core and apex group and had invested time and effort to see this movement blossom. Their involvement in many ways provided much-needed attention to detail in the formative years. This is what great leaders do. They invest their time in building excellence across an organisation.

PRISM AND REFRACTIONS

This story would be incomplete without taking a peek at Tata Steel from the late 1980s. Tata Steel was already on a path of excellence under the leadership of Dr. Jamshed Irani and had a first mover's advantage in adopting the Baldrige criteria for continuous improvements through disciplined and well organised internal assessments for its various divisions, including Mines, Collieries, Town, Health, and the Strategic Business Units.

The reservoir of talent from Tata Steel was a welcome addition to this mix and the board members encouraged and supported collaboration across the Tata Group. Excellence is about going from strength to strength.

The enormous talent that resided in Tata Steel and its subsidiary companies brought many talented people aboard the excellence ship that Ratan Tata, JK Setna, SA Vaneswaran, and Raghu Kalé had built from 1995 to 1997. Jamshed Daboo of Titan Industries took over as second CEO from SA Vaneswaran, and then I had an opportunity to move from Tata Steel in 2000 to be the third CEO of Tata Quality Management Services. Dr. Jamshed Irani became the second Chairman of the Executive Council to head Tata Quality Management Services in 2002. When I moved to a new challenge in 2002 with higher responsibilities to become the Executive Vice President and Global Head of Business Excellence for Tata Consultancy Services, Jehangir Ardeshir joined as the fourth CEO. The fifth CEO, Sunil Sinha, took charge in 2005. Both Jehangir and Sunil came with several years of experience at Tata Steel.

Each CEO of Tata Quality Management Services brought his own strengths, specialities, and strategic improvements in the Excellence Model and the assessment process. For example, I had introduced the concept of a Mentor, a very senior executive, at the level of CXO, to be part of the assessment team, to guide and bring in the business perspective in the assessment process. This not only improved the team's assessment but also brought an improvement in the feedback report. Another big advantage was the Mentors showed sincere commitment to the Tata Business Excellence Model as they were expected to guide the assessment team. This resulted in designing special training programmes for the 'to be mentors' from different group companies. The byproduct was a much better understanding among group companies and their executives who participated as mentors.

The Tata Business Excellence seed was well sown, and the foundation laid was becoming stronger by the end of every year, with the loving care of a dedicated team of Tata Quality Management Services and well-nourished with proper nutrients from the Tata leadership. It turned out that Tatas had finally acquired a successful banyan tree that ensured continuous improvements and overall commitment to excellence through the Tata Business Excellence Model and the JRD Quality Value Award.

As I write this, the Tata Business Excellence Model has celebrated its silver jubilee and has helped the group achieve its global aspirations of growth and sustained excellence. This was possible because Ratan Tata and the other top leadership made the long-term goals crystal clear.

STRATEGIC GOAL UNVEILED

At the first JRD Quality Value Awards Function in 1995, Ratan Tata said that if the Tata Group must face a highly competitive environment in the future and if the group's name should stand above that of its competitors, then Tatas must become market-oriented, much more driven to go beyond customers' needs, conscious of the quality of its products and services, and more importantly, conscious, and aware of the quality of business processes.

For five long years, Tata Quality Management Services carried out assessments meticulously and could not find a company that surpassed the threshold of the criteria for the award. The Executive Council of Tata Quality Management Services decided that the JRD Quality Value Award should be given, if and only if, the assessed company scored 600+ points overall out of a maximum of 1,000 points. This was in line with international benchmarks prevailing at that time. A few CEOs from the group companies saw strong improvements in the categories of customer and workforce engagements, process improvements in leadership communications, strategy development, and climate change initiatives. The results corroborated the process improvements. However, the JRDQV award was not given as the benchmark threshold was not crossed by any of the companies. One of the CEOs even suggested that the criteria standards needed to be lowered to enable the companies to win the award. However, Ratan Tata stood strong on his principle and did not yield to such an idea and fully supported the Tata Business Excellence Model and its rigorous assessment process.

The breakthrough came when Tata Steel, under the leadership of Dr. Jamshed Irani won the coveted JRD Quality Value Award in 2000. Ratan Tata addressed the entire group leadership team on the 29th July 2001 during the JRD Quality Value Awards function held at the Taj Mahal Hotel, Mumbai. I am humbled that I was hosting the meet in my capacity as the CEO of Tata Quality Management Services on JRD's 97th birth anniversary. Here are a few excerpts from that powerful address:

> *"It's very important for us to realise that the world is moving at a tremendous pace. Many of our companies have not moved fast enough and many of our people still don't see the need for change. Where we can change is to have something to guide that change. And that change must be embodied through people and processes. When we started this process, some of us, and certainly I, felt frustrated because I sensed a great deal of cynicism, many people who thought all this was unnecessary, that it was just a fad. Nothing has pleased me more than to sit here today and see that an idea to which we gave birth five years ago has blossomed into something that hopefully will be one of the driving forces of change in the group.*

> *Last year at this time, it was a matter of great happiness to see one of our company's (Tata Steel) finally win the JRD Quality Value Award. I think Jamshed (Dr. Jamshed J Irani) and his team deserves every bit of the acknowledgement they received on that occasion."*

The Executive Council of Tata Quality Management Services had decided that a company winning the award for the first time will not be eligible for the award a second time but would be encouraged to get themselves assessed to monitor their improvement process. Bringing this important point to the attention of the CEOs present, Ratan Tata made his point.

"The Tata Steel people could have taken a holiday from this whole process (this year) since they knew they could not win the award again, that being what we had decided. But it is really gratifying to see that the company decided to stay with this process and continued to work at it. As Jaggu (the author) said, this is a journey that really has no end."

He concluded his emotionally charged and inspiring address by saying:

"The Tata Group has a tremendous resource: you and your colleagues in this room, and those outside in several of our companies. The greatest thing we can do is to marshal and direct this synergistic resource to make our group stand out far above the rest of the businesses in this country. We need to strive for excellence, and we have a process before us that will help make this happen ... I really believe that the Tata Group has much to gain from this process in the years to come." [2d]

Ratan Tata was so right. When he stepped down from the chairmanship of the group in 2012, he had the best financials for the group to boast of, with all key processes in benchmark positions, worldwide. During his tenure as chairman of the group from 1991 till he retired in 2012, the revenue and profits went up

40 and 50 times respectively! He built on the strong foundations of the founder's values, business ethics set by his predecessors, and catapulted the growth engine to a formidable speed. An excellent record for Excellence!

DEVELOPING EXCELLENCE

Excellence is an attitude that can be developed. It is relatively easy to build a positive attitude in small children and even to make them appreciate excellence in work at an early age. Even when someone is older it is still possible to develop a better attitude by following the five steps which I have used over the years with success. These steps are neither sequential nor interdependent.

One — Benchmarking: After my second semester exams in Grade 8, way back in 1962, I was calculating my total marks and working out my overall percentage score during the school recess. It worked out to 76%. *"Wow. That's great!"*, I thought. The system of education was very different in those days. It was very difficult to score even 60%, which was considered an 'A' Grade by today's standards. Exams were very tough, unlike the way schools test the students these days. I did not realise that there was someone standing behind me, who said, *"That's not enough. You should aim for at least 80-85% if you want to be in the Merit List of the Top 20 amongst approximately 60,000 students who appear for the Higher Secondary School Certification Exam (equivalent to the Grade XII final school exams across the entire county in the USA)."* My Science

Teacher (the late) MS Kharkanis, who taught us Maths and Physics, was behind me and made that observation.

That shocked me. On further exploration with him, I found that our school turned out great students, and there was at least one student every year in the Merit List of the HSSCE. Their average score was around 82%. He set in my mind a benchmark score that I should aim for and exceed if I wanted to excel academically. I broke down the average percentage score and found that in science subjects I should score full or better marks as these are more objective evaluations as compared to subjective evaluations in languages and social studies. I did hit the Merit list at the HSSCE in 1965. Thanks to my teacher who set the benchmark for me!

Two — Good Company: My parents taught me, time and time again, to choose my friends carefully as they believed that this matters a lot in life. It was almost daily routine advice. In my primary and middle school days, I had not paid much attention to this. But it dawned on me that I should surround myself with people who were brilliant and more intelligent than I was. The idea, I thought resonated well with Step One — Benchmarking. This necessitated to extending friendship across grades and even schools. I recall I had many friends from higher as well as lower grades. Some friends were from different schools. One of them, junior to me in grade, had never known what it was to be ranked no. 2, and I learnt newer ways of learning a subject and answering exams from him.

Three — A Role Model / Mentor: Look for someone who is held high in your esteem and who has had a great impact in your early life. They could be characters from scriptural stories or great people like the few we discussed in the earlier chapter on Humility. These are the people who make you shed joyful tears and say, *"Yes, I want to be like him or her".* They influence us not because of their background or wealth, position of power, colour, or race, but because of what they think, say, and do. Their actions speak for them. Read, think, contemplate, and put into practice the lessons learnt from them. Discuss with your friends your role model and what made you decide that he or she is your role model, irrespective of their field. It does not matter whether they are scientists, doctors, athletes, politicians, musicians, or spiritual leaders, it is important that they are exemplary in their fields.

A role model will kindle the dormant force of excellence in us and will help nourish and sustain a positive attitude, and their actions will provide us guidance when faced with challenges. This book gives several examples of role models based on actual experiences.

Four — Learning From Nature: Seasons come and go. The Sun rises and sets (or rather the earth revolves around the sun!). Trees grow and die. You may ask what is there for me to learn from nature about excellence? Spending a few minutes every day in natural surroundings is not only refreshing and relaxing but also educational. Nature is filled with examples of excellence in any direction you walk. Be it the buzzing bees in search of fresh flowers to collect their honey, or the ducks quacking and swimming in the cold waters of a lake, or thousands of ants forming a line, carrying grain to their homes in the anthill; it is simply an awesome sight. They all teach teamwork, divided execution with responsibility, and excellent communication. Most importantly they have never been seen fighting with each other. It is cooperation, good understanding, discipline, and teamwork all the way.

The Ants' Palace! — I had an opportunity to see an inside view of an anthill in 1969. It was mind-boggling. The ants had built an awesome palace with halls, chambers, and balconies. How did they engineer the design, instruct their fellow ants to carry out the job plan, and finish their work without any blueprint? The architecture and construction clearly show all the elements of passion, planning, perseverance, effective communication, teamwork, and most importantly, to excel in what they were doing silently. We have something to learn!

The Home on a Hanger — Same is true of the nests built by birds. The Baya weaver (Ploceus philippinus) is famous for its nest. I had learned that the male weaves an interlocking structure that gives strength and stability using blades of grass. It suspends the nest from the thorny branch of a tree. When I saw the nest, I wondered how this small weaver bird could construct a suspended house all by itself without a visual plan? A true engineering marvel. Of course, we know the intricacy of a beehive. I wonder how many bee-hours it must take to build a house that supports hundreds of bees and produces several pounds of honey collected from many different flowers and gardens? Mind you, every one of the homes discussed is eco-friendly!

Nature is boundless and yet Humble — Looking at the vast Pacific Ocean on the West Coast of the USA, the magnificent Isuzu Falls in Argentina, the rainforest of the Amazon in Brazil, and the snow-clad mountains of the Himalayas, the viewer is thrilled, and a warm joyous feeling runs through him. That feeling cannot be photographed or expressed in words. We feel humbled and so small when compared to the mighty oceans and the lofty mountains. They all teach us to practise humility in our lives and provoke us to see the excellence around us. Nature keeps giving all the time and has always forgiven our past mistakes of acting on greed, tampering with her by polluting the air and water, felling trees, and the sheer abuse of natural resources. When natural calamities attack the lives of all beings, we are simply helpless. We cannot stop a tsunami or an earthquake. Accumulated abuse results in unleashing the fury of nature.

A mango seed grows to become a tree to give flowers and then mango fruits. Not one but in the hundreds. The same is true for an orange or an apple seed. When we look at the seed, we don't realise what is hidden. Inside that little seed lies huge potential that can grow and give excellent results. So also, the trait of excellence lies inside each one of us. It is our important duty to awaken this quality, allow it to blossom, and make every act of ours suffused with excellence.

Five — Perseverance: I also realised that perseverance is a key ingredient. It is best illustrated by Thomas Alva Edison, the monarch of inventors. He said, *"Our greatest weakness lies in giving up. The most certain way to succeed is always to try just one more time!"*

Every Failure Takes Us One Step Closer to Success

You are waitlisted! — The year was 1978. Mr. Homi Bodhanwala, Director of Tata Steel, saw me in his office on a Sunday morning, in Jamshedpur. I was at that time with Tata Motors in the same city. The reason for the meeting was that I had applied for a Rotary International Award titled 'Group Study Exchange Program (GSE)' that year. I became qualified after two selection rounds for the final interview. As luck would have it, I was not selected by the interview panel. I was placed first on the waiting list.

The GSE of Rotary International was one of the best for those in the age group of 25 to 35 years. The five most competent professionals were selected from a Rotary District (a Rotary District is different from the districts designated by the Government for administrative purposes). The team of five, under the leadership of a past President of one of the Rotary Clubs, was sponsored to visit another Rotary District, usually in another country. The programme duration was for a period of six weeks with the idea to promote goodwill and understanding. The five selected young men were called 'Goodwill Ambassadors' of the district. It was mandatory that the five men selected should not be in any way related to members of the Rotary Clubs. This was one of the most prestigious awards in the 1970s and 80s.

It is ironic that I was first on the waiting list even in the previous year when I had applied for the award in 1976-77. I was asked to fill in lengthy forms for a visa, travel documents, and details related to health, meal preferences, and emergency contacts. I sincerely followed the process but could not make it. Based on my last experience, I declined to accept the offer and fill out all the forms again in 1978.

When I entered the office of Homi Bodhanwalla, I realised that he was a very simple, straightforward man, and he wasted no time, nor minced his words. After the initial courtesies were exchanged, he got to the point. He said, *"Jagannathan, why are you refusing to sign the documents for the visa application as you have every chance of going as a member of the GSE team if one of the five members is not able to make it?"* I thought to myself, *"OMG, here again, I have to explain the whole episode."* I gathered my courage and said, *"Sir, frankly speaking, I have lost confidence in the selection process."* Homi was shocked. He was the Chairman of the selection panel in 1977-78 and was well known for adhering to high human values of righteousness, truthfulness, and integrity. He was the President of the Rotary Club of Jamshedpur in 1973-74 and was very popular in Rotary District 325. I remember that he was so fair that when my turn came for the interview he got up and left the room saying, *"Jagannathan is a candidate from Jamshedpur and my presence on the panel should not influence the decision of the other panellists. So, I will exclude myself from this particular interview."*

He said, *"I am surprised that you are saying this. Could you be more specific?"* I said, "Sure," and continued. I went on non-stop with my monologue.

"Sir, after you left the interview room, the panellists asked me some general questions about my professional accomplishments and various other interests. Just as I thought the interview was ending, the panelists glanced at each other and one of them asked me about my native language. I replied that it was Tamil (one of the languages spoken predominantly in the state of Tamil Nadu, South India). Immediately another member wanted to know the city I was born in. I said I was born in Nagpur, Maharashtra State. (The city is located almost in the centre of India.) Another panellist almost concluded and said that since I speak Tamil, and was born in Nagpur, I should have applied for this programme either from Tamil Nadu or from Maharashtra and not from the state of Bihar. (Jamshedpur city was then part of Bihar. From the year 2000, it became part of Jharkhand State). The other panellists agreed. I was not surprised but shocked. I said the application requires that candidates should be professionally qualified, in good standing, and should have a minimum of three years of professional experience. I think I satisfy all the conditions extremely well."

Homi was silent throughout while I was talking and was listening with utmost alacrity. Finally, he said, *"I am sorry to hear that. However, that is no reason to give up and not fill out the necessary forms as a wait-listed candidate."* Looking at my hesitation he gave me one of the greatest lessons in perseverance. He went into great detail about the lives of Abraham Lincoln, Mahatma Gandhi, Swami Vivekananda, and Jamsetji Tata and how they never accepted defeat but persevered until they succeeded. He reminded me of the famous quote of Swami Vivekananda, *"Arise, Awake, stop not till the goal is reached."* He asked me to study the life history of Abe Lincoln and said that Lincoln was the record holder of failures and success at the same time. He presented me with a book on Mahatma Gandhi and urged me to read it. He said, *"If I were you, I wouldn't give up,"* and gave me the forms to sign. He had planned this meeting to last 45 minutes, but he extended it by another 45 minutes with his convincing examples and anecdotes from the great leaders' lives. He showed me, with full clarity, that success follows when a person, with a single-pointed focus, pools all his energy and never gives up.

His emotional and inspirational presentation was so convincing that I signed the papers and resolved that I would not give up, come what may. The wait-listed position was not of much use that year. However, I applied again, the very next year (1978-79), and went through the same process. I am happy to write that I was selected as the Goodwill Ambassador and became a member of the GSE team. I visited Rotary District 552 in Texas and part of New Mexico, USA. I had one of the best cultural and professional experiences of my life. What I observed and learnt in those six weeks is equivalent to two years of learning from any management institute, anywhere in the world. I learnt that unconditional love is the foundation for international peace; cultural differences, and differences in human behaviour could be overcome through goodwill and understanding. Thanks to Rotary International for the opportunity, and to Homi Bodhanwalla, who counselled and instilled in me the value of perseverance.

Failure and Success Record Holder! — Since Homi mentioned Abraham Lincoln, the 16th President of the USA, it is topical to briefly reflect on his life. He is one of the most respected and revered Presidents of the USA to date. His success story is remarkable and could be considered equivalent to a great epic. However, would you ever imagine that Lincoln could have faced defeat, one after another, before success even touched his feet?

His failures were numerous, and he went through several hardships in life that could have led one to total and ruinous depression. He lost eight elections and failed in business twice. But he never gave up. His perseverance was probably the best quality that captures everyone's attention. *2e*

Never Give Up — Another great leader who strongly believed in the age-old saying, 'Try, try, try again', based on the famous poem about Robert Bruce, is Sir Winston Churchill. He led his country during World War II as the UK's Prime Minister. After the war, he was invited by his school as the Guest of Honour and invited to deliver the keynote address at the school's 150th celebrations. Referring to this speech, Lt. Gen (Ret.) Dr. M. L. Chibber writes in his book:

"On the appointed day, the hall where the function was being held was overflowing with people. The media and the scholars had turned up in strength. Everyone was looking forward to Sir Winston Churchill revealing the secrets of his leadership. After the usual courtesies, Churchill was invited to deliver the keynote address. He got up from his chair, walked slowly to the podium, took out small rectangular glasses and wore them. He then took out a small piece of paper, placed it on the podium and peered over his glasses at the audience. There was pin-drop silence. He then delivered his address:

'Never, Never, Never, Never, Give Up,'

Having roared these five words, he walked back to his seat. There was a bewildered hush for a long time. However, his great message soon sank home. People stood up and gave him a long and thunderous ovation."[2f]

Do I need to say anymore?

My personal experience of trying out these valuable steps clearly shows that it works. Excellence can be developed and should begin at home and at the primary school level. If children of today are infused with ideas of excellence and embedded with an attitude of exceeding their own performance, at every level, then the future for them is a guaranteed success. Parents must become role models before they ask their children to act in a certain way. We will focus more on this in the next chapter titled 'Action'.

TAKEAWAYS

1. Desire to excel stems from within. It is an attitude based on what we value most.
2. Business Excellence can be developed by setting up a process for excellence. The process, however, requires unconditional support and active participation from the head of the organisation.
3. Excellence can be developed by consciously paying attention to the following five steps:
   i. Benchmarking.
   ii. Good company.
   iii. Role Models / Mentors.
   iv. Learning from Nature.
   v. Perseverance.

REFLECTIONS

1. Is excellence necessary to be a great leader? Why is this so important?
2. Would I ever follow a leader who accepts a shoddy job and doesn't recognise or demand excellent work?
3. Do I believe that people will follow my instructions and my way of doing a job even if I don't follow it myself?
4. How do I instill the quality of excellence in me, my friends, and colleagues at my workplace?
5. What steps do I have to take to achieve excellence?

*You are
what you do,*

*not what you say
you'll do.*

— Carl Gustav Jung

3. WHEN YOU DO – IT HAPPENS

I saw them in action

Over the years, I have seen how intentions get diluted. Despite many professionals working for a common cause, the results are lacking. Here is a case in point based on a real situation I witnessed, reflected on, and wondered about. To protect the persons involved identities, I have changed their names to Jim Walters and Vikram Das. The essence of the story is not in their names but in what they did.

Jim Walters, the CEO, and Vikram Das the COO ran a software company called 'Actions Unlimited'. Initially started as a small company with a highly dedicated workforce, it grew through two mergers and acquisitions. They were engaged in the design of special products for which the global market potential was estimated to be around $4 billion. The company got stuck in the sales revenue graveyard of $400-420 million for well over three years. On the other hand, the global market for their products and services grew at 15%, year-on-year, over the same period. Obviously, their competitors were having a good time.

The company's leadership team met, every year, at an exotic resort for three days and discussed strategies to improve revenues and profits. Jim Walters, the CEO was in his mid-60s and had a unique style of leadership. He delegated more than a normal

CEO would do and gave complete independence to his COO, Vikram Das. Vikram was young and courteous. He had completed his MBA from one of the highly reputed universities in the USA and was in India. He arranged for experts from the industry to come and address the leadership team and consulted with them on the business potential and how it was likely to grow in the subsequent five years. Every expert, without exception, suggested an increase in business revenue, for the industry, by at least $4 billion. World-renowned consultants, who were also engaged to help in strategy formulation, confirmed similar numbers in revenue growth over the same time frame.

After many deliberations, the strategy worked out was a two-pronged one: doubling sales (revenue) in three years through organic growth of 15%, year-on-year, giving $210 million extra revenue, and through mergers and acquisitions to provide the balance of $200 million. Vikram and two of his favourite team members worked out the details and responsibilities and did not think it necessary to discuss with others.

The CEO of the strategy consulting company, in his concluding remarks said, *"The secret of success lies in strategy execution rather than in strategic planning as there exists a high growth potential. All economic indicators confirm this growth potential."*

Everybody cheered at the end of the meet, promised one another that they would help each other, and achieve well over the targets. However, once they all returned to their respective workplaces, everything related to targets was conveniently either forgotten or ignored except the caviar and champagne they had at the resort. The industry achieved the growth of an additional 15%, but Actions Unlimited had their revenues increased by 10% organically. M&A remained on the paper in thick blue folders that carried the caption 'strictly confidential' on the top right-hand corner!

The action was lacking. Someone who attended the company's strategy meets over three years jokingly remarked, *"We are not Actions Unlimited but Inaction Unlimited."*

> *Passion is truly a secret ingredient —*
> *One can't buy it. One cannot outsource it.*

DEMAND THE BEST AND PEOPLE WILL DO THE REST

Let me contrast this anecdote with another case where the bias for action was remarkably high, resulting in tremendous success, year after year.

Another global IT software and services company had their annual budget planning starting sometime in October of every year. The company's financial year was from 1st April to 31st March of the following year. The US geography held the lion's share of the total business revenue for this company. The Head of US Operations was expected to discuss with his direct reports and present a robust plan to the VP of Sales and Strategy, and the CEO. The VP of Sales and Strategy directly reported to the CEO. Targets were firmed up after the plan was approved.

In the year 2003, the meeting was convened in the first week of October. The CEO and VP came to New York from Mumbai for a face-to-face meeting. The idea was to discuss with the team of senior executives from the US geography, understand their perspectives, expectations, and set a realistic and yet challenging target for the next year. The team had developed plans, independently, for their respective divisions.

Every one of them, without exception, had fallen into the 10% growth syndrome. The team pegged targets at 10% more than the previous year. The CEO, after patiently hearing the team said, *"I did not come here to learn that you will perform 10% better than last year. I am sorry, you have not done your homework at all. I don't want to hear anymore."*

He stopped the meeting abruptly and just walked out. This shocked everyone in the room. No one had seen the CEO so upset in the recent history of the company. The VP also left with him but promised to come back after about half an hour. That gap of thirty minutes was the most anxious moment the team had ever experienced. The team conjectured on what would happen next. *"Would the bosses come back? Are we supposed to rework the targets? Would some of us be fired?"* The geography head and his whole team of managers were looking at their approach and rechecking all their calculations. The mindset was such that they were still not willing to venture and commit to higher numbers.

In the meanwhile, the VP returned to discuss further. He was the master of details and numbers and was very thorough in his work.

He was always well prepared and had the facts and figures at his fingertips. Based on his study of the geography he said, *"The boss is very upset, and he doesn't want to come back, unless the team does a thorough job and commits itself for more ambitious targets, instead of taking safe routes."* He further explained, taking one industry vertical as an example, to show how much potential exists for business growth. Looking at all the strengths and weaknesses, opportunities, and threats, he presented that the business growth could not be just 10%, but probably 65% more than that of last year. He was so lucid and logical in his arguments that it was very difficult to challenge him on those numbers. The team was wonderstruck.

Having explained, he asked, *"Any questions? Any clarifications?"* There was pin-drop silence. Finally, he said, "I'll come back after an hour. You know more about the US market and the competitors than I do. Carry out a realistic analysis and then give your figures." With a gentle smile, he left the conference room.

That set the ball rolling for the team in the room to reset and re-evaluate their methodology. The team worked through the critical gaps and came back with the figures dramatically increased.

The VP came back after two hours, giving the team more time to think and come up with better work. Finally, when he returned, the average increase stood out at almost 35% more, and in some cases even as high as 65%. That was probably more acceptable. In the evening, the CEO came with a smile saying, *"I am pleased that you have reworked the numbers. Do you agree with these numbers?"* Everyone in the room agreed. He continued, *"We need to put our best foot forward and aim for achieving the goal, harnessing our highest potential. I know you will surely achieve your committed targets."*

One stern remonstration and assertive behaviour showed that the boss meant business. It was clear that no targets were fixed by the boss, but by the people in the field. There was more commitment to those numbers, which would improve the probability of achieving the target. The leader's communication was clear: Conviction commands commitment.

The VP was a great taskmaster. Yet, a human touch encouraged and helped the team to achieve their targets. Both the CEO and the VP showed a high bias for action. They set up a culture of Execution Excellence throughout the organisation that is seen even two decades later.

HUMAN TOUCH CANNOT BE FAKED

The CEO was none other than S. Ramadorai, and the VP was N. Chandrasekaran (more popularly known as Chandra). Chandra took the reins of Tata Consultancy Services from Ramadorai in 2009 and is currently the chairman of Tata Group, India's most globalised conglomerate. Ram, Chandra, and the leadership team of Tata Consultancy Services followed this philosophy, 'Bias for Action' in letter and spirit. No wonder Tata Consultancy Services achieved its vision of becoming *'Top 10 by 2010'* one year in advance!

Great leaders ensure the harmony of their thoughts, words, and actions. Dr. Martin Luther King said, *"Great leaders know that they must stay focused on their mission if they want their teams to follow suit."*

DIFFICULT COLLEAGUE

"We need to start training programmes on business excellence, and the sole objective is to make everybody aware of the Tata Business Excellence guidelines, and the Assessment criteria," I said during the meeting with the head of US Operations at Tata Consultancy Services in New York. I had joined Tata Consultancy Services on the 6th February 2002 in Mumbai. After my initial induction in India, I took charge of my office in Santa Clara, California, later in the month. After coming to the US, I met the VP and head of the US Operations and set up a meeting with him to discuss the roll-out plan for Tata Business Excellence Model. I discussed my plans and explained to him the step-by-step approach in driving Business Excellence. He replied, *"Yes, yes, definitely, you can conduct any training programme you want, but please do it during the weekends."* This was a very different proposal, and I was quite ill-prepared for this. I said, *"Weekends?"* He said, *"Yes, weekends only, as all the officers and managers are busy during the weekdays."*

I quickly made my strategic chess moves and weighed the pros and cons mentally and said, *"That's okay with me, provided associates will come during the weekends."* He said without even blinking, *"Well, that's your responsibility to make the training programmes interesting and attractive. Make sure they come to the programmes.*

But as far as I'm concerned, I know that this is important, but you should conduct the training only during the weekends."

Thirty years of corporate experience had taught me that battles are not won by simple arguments. There are several other approaches to win. I then said, *"It's a big task, but surely I will do my best. To show that the US leadership team is committed to Excellence, I would like to have the first programme with you and your team. You have to come to the first programme, inaugurate it and speak on the importance of this approach."* He became a little uncomfortable but responded saying, *"I will try, but I can't promise."* That was not what I expected. The pull and push started again and went on for some more time and he was not willing to yield. Without losing my cool, I assertively said, *"I would only like to start when you say you are participating with all your direct reports. The leadership team has to set an example."* He looked at me with surprise as he had not expected this from me. *"I cannot promise,"* he replied and was getting up to leave. I continued my plea saying, *"You choose the date, time and venue and give me just four hours. That's all I need."* However, he was adamant. As the situation was leading nowhere, I assertively said, *"In that case, I can't start the programme here in the US."* I left, heading out to board my flight to San Jose, CA.

Looking at the drifting clouds out of my window seat on my flight to San Jose, my thoughts drifted as I saw the jet engines attached to the wing and that give the plane its lift. Flights take off when the integrity of the powerful engine is taken for granted. Nothing worthwhile can be achieved if the engine is not running the way it is supposed to function. What if a direct approach has not worked? Is there a way to achieve a smooth flight with a stuttering engine? I pressed the '*Refresh*' key on my mental computer and the answer popped up – we need a massive gust of wind from below! I wondered if I should nudge the 'higher authority' to provide this lift? Then we could glide, and the engines would stutter and start. I was travelling to India in March for a meeting with our CEO, and to initiate the programmes in India. I knew exactly what had to be done.

The Boss' Commitment

When I came to India and met our CEO, Ramadorai, he asked me, *"How is it going in the US?"* I said, *"Pretty tough."* I narrated the face-to-face meeting I had with the Head of US Operations, his reluctance, and the outcome. Ram listened to me very carefully until I finished and then said, *"Yes, I quite understand that the first programme has to start with the leadership team to show their commitment to the new initiative. What we could do is ..."* He paused for a moment and said, *"I am visiting New York in two weeks. Can you organise a training programme at that time so that I will be available to attend it?"* Without blinking an eye, the CEO knew exactly what was needed. I was happy to see the positive approach and his readiness to help the cause of Excellence. I quickly showed the Business Excellence Awareness Programme plan and requested him to inaugurate the programme. I also added that it would be for about four hours. *"Four hours, okay,"* he said, as he looked at his diary. *"I arrive in New York in the afternoon, and you can plan for the programme at 3 PM. Book the Taj Lexington Hotel for the programme."* I said, *"Thank you, Sir, for your support. I'll go ahead and arrange this programme."*

I came back to the USA and made all the arrangements. Invitations were sent to the entire Leadership team of Tata Consultancy Services in the USA. I also called the head of US Operations and casually informed him that Ram has agreed to inaugurate and attend the programme as well. *"Would you be able to attend this programme?"* I asked. I could imagine the shock he received. *"I will surely come, and I will make sure that my team is also present,"* he said.

Every one of his direct reports signed up for the programme, and the CEO's presence assured full attendance. For those four hours, the CEO gave his full attention and did not leave his chair. He was the best participant in the room. At the end of the meeting, the CEO said, *"Look, it is very important that we understand the criteria, what this business excellence model means to us and are committed to driving our business as per the Tata Business Excellence Model. The sooner we adopt this model into our processes and working, the better it will be for all of us. Do I get a commitment from all of you?"* Everybody, without exception, said, *"Yes!"* He then looked at me and said, *"Jaggu, you have the team's commitment. And you can go ahead and implement all the things that you discussed with me earlier, and make sure that everybody follows. If not, let me know."* And with that, he closed the meeting and left.

People were wondering how Ram found so much time and so keenly participated in the meeting. The value of the meeting automatically went up in their minds. The team guaranteed its commitment. In 2004, within just two years, Tata Consultancy Services won the JRD Quality Value Award, which was the benchmark for Excellence in the Tata Group. Tata Steel had won the award in the year 2000, and it had taken them almost five years of concentrated effort. Whereas Tata Consultancy Services, even though globally widespread, took just two years to achieve that same award.

It is possible to move elephants and make them dance, provided the leader is committed and shows the steps in an exemplary manner. Actions speak for themselves!

WHAT IS ACTION?

In my very close association with several successful CEOs of the Tata Group, I found that *'bias for action'* runs as a common attribute for all of them. Action, no doubt means work, steps, measures, and many more. It also means the persistence of the following six attributes in these leaders:

1. Accomplishment.
2. Communication.
3. Task clarity.
4. Information validity.
5. Organisation culture, and
6. Never give up attitude.

Action, as we saw, is the physical demonstration of the leader, either in supporting or taking steps in the direction of the goals to be accomplished. For example, during the 2008 global financial crisis, several steps were taken by Tata Consultancy Services to reduce costs. One of them was travel expenses. Voluntarily, Ramadorai and his direct reports decided to travel by economy class instead of business class for all domestic flights.

Secondly, communication was amplified several times by the actions leaders undertook. They strongly believed that actions loudly conveyed the leader's message without speaking! Verbal communication is difficult to retain and is easily forgotten. But actions leave a deep impression on the mind. Besides, what they communicated was not vague but crystal clear. Their expectations were very carefully articulated and expressed at the right time to have the maximum impact.

Thirdly, the leaders could speak with precision because of task clarity. The goal was clear to them, and every action had been detailed in a focused manner based on facts.

Fourthly, the in-depth knowledge was gathered and checked for the validity of information in advance, through discussions with stakeholders and experts. They were not shy to learn from juniors. A willingness to learn was high. They were excellent listeners.

Repeated practise of the above four steps, at every level of the organisation, builds confidence and sets the foundations for action-driven organisational culture, the fifth step.

A 'never give up attitude' is the sixth step, and which we discussed in the previous chapter, strengthens the organisational culture of bias for action.

HOME VIS-A-VIS OFFICE

Many times, I have wondered whether it is possible to adapt or replicate the actions one takes in home management in the corporate world. At home, what do we do when we want to save money for a luxury cruise to Alaska? We prepare a plan, estimate the budget, and if there is a cash crunch, we start to put aside a certain amount of dollars every day, week, or month. Savings must be action-driven, prompt, swift, and monitored. We start immediately. But what happens in the corporate world?

REDUCE THE BUDGET

In 1979, I had the privilege of visiting Germany to visit the Sindelfingen Plant of Daimler Benz, the auto giant, and a few nearby auto ancillaries. I was then with Tata Motors, Jamshedpur, India. And one of the visits was to Mahle Pistons, a world-class automotive piston manufacturer. While there were several systems and technical processes worth emulating, I would like to highlight the point that is relevant here.

What attracted me was their suggestion box system. The company encouraged their employees to give suggestions for cost, productivity, process, and quality improvements. They had a strict process of evaluating proposals. Once the suggestion was accepted by the management, the concerned department immediately implemented it. The executive who was explaining the whole process of the suggestion scheme to me said that the implementation starts almost instantly. I was very surprised.

We also had a suggestion box system in Tata Motors, which was very good, and many times nationally recognised. However, as a member of the suggestion box committee, I always found that the time for implementing a suggestion was very long.

So, I asked, *"How do you manage that? What is the process that reduces the implementation time?"*

He replied, *"It's quite simple. We calculate the benefit of the suggestion in terms of Deutschmarks. The expected amount of savings is reduced from the budget of the department for the year. Take, for example, the financial year was from 1st April 1976 to 31st March 1977.*

Let us assume that the suggestion got implemented in December 1976. Then January, February, and March would be the three months where the benefits would accrue during the financial year 1976-77.

So, for those three months, whatever was the benefit, the CFO deducted the exact amount from the cost budget of that specific department.

So, there's even more reason why the department head would be keen to implement the suggestion in the fastest manner."

The budget reduction idea, I thought, was a compelling one and an excellent way to make sure the implementations are practical. It is direct action that gets results.

ACTIONS SPEAK LOUDER THAN WORDS

"The most important thing I learned is that soldiers watch what their leaders do. You can give them classes and lecture them forever, but it is your example they will follow." – General Colin Powell.

Have you faced the challenge of almost losing your job because of a promotion that you got?

I did. It was the 16th September 1996, when we were holding the Apex Quality Council (AQC) Meeting at Tata Steel. Dr. Jamshed J Irani, the CEO, was in the chair. We had all the members of the council, like the Vice Presidents of various functions, such as Operations, R & D, Sales & Marketing, Central Engineering & Projects, HR, and Administration, and the Total Quality Management Team were present. As head of the Total Quality and Reengineering Division, I was presenting the report we had received on the assessment of the company from the Tata Quality Management Services. The assessment was carried out as per the Tata Business Excellence Model. We had performed very poorly.

Tata Steel's low score was shocking to everyone. The financial results were always good. In 1995-96, the company had gone through the first assessment as per the Tata Business Excellence Model.

The first point in the agenda was to study and understand the feedback report. I had the tough task of presenting the report in my very first Apex Quality Council Meeting. The very first point, the feedback report with a very low overall score was a terrible blow to everyone present. Dr. Irani was visibly upset. He asked, *"What went wrong, and who is responsible for this?"* His tone reflected anger and frustration. There was pin-drop silence in the room, and no one wanted to answer or take responsibility. I had just taken over on the 1st September, that year, as the head of the Total Quality and Reengineering Division. I was only fifteen days in that role.

Everybody in the meeting knew that I wasn't responsible, but somebody had to answer. The CEO was very upset, and he asked again, *"Who is responsible for this?"* Listening to the silence again, I decided to take the risk. I said, *"All of us are responsible."* He stopped me, and asked *"What do you mean, all of us are responsible?"* I said, *"Yes, Sir, all of us, because none of us have understood the criteria of the Tata Business Excellence Model, and the assessment process."* He said, *"Can you explain?"* By this time, he had cooled off. I explained the criteria very, very briefly, and I said, *"We must thoroughly understand the criteria guidelines, and prepare well before we ask for an assessment."*

After listening to what I had said, Dr. Irani asked, *"What should we do to understand the requirements of the criteria?"* He was seeking clarifications and suggestions and I thought my fear of losing the new elevated position was unnecessary. I replied, *"We need a training programme for at least two days. We need to go through all the seven criteria of the Tata Business Excellence guidebook."*

Remembering that the criteria guidelines used a rather complicated language I added, *"This training programme has to be conducted by someone who is very familiar with the criteria and who can explain lucidly to all of us in a simple language".*

"If you need two days for the training programme, then I will give you my dates just now," Dr. Irani said while looking in his red diary, which he always carried with him. He flipped through the pages and indicated two consecutive dates in November 1996. He said, *"Please book the Dimna Training Center, and I will be available on both these dates. Arrange a faculty, get somebody who is hands-on and can explain it well. I'm willing to invest two days for this."* Then he asked the million-dollar question. *"Who else is willing to come for this programme from this Apex Quality Council?"* He raised his hand himself. Looking at the boss, everyone else, including all the VPs and senior executives raised their hands saying that they would also commit. I fixed the date, and we had the CEO of Tata Quality Management Services, S A Vaneswaran, explain the criteria to the management team in the November of 1996.

Dr. Irani showed his commitment by attending the training programme as an active participant. He demonstrated his willingness to go along with the requirements, understand them, and apply them. The very next year, the application we submitted scored more than 400 points which showed a 100% increase, because of our understanding of the subject. Dr. Irani's wholehearted commitment, repeated communication, and never give up spirit helped Tata Steel to steer the Business Excellence movement in the company. No wonder Tata Steel became the first company in the Tata Group to win the JRDQV Award for Business Excellence in the year 2000.

When Dr. Irani took over as CEO of Tata Steel in 1992, he had listed 13 actions, which he called 'What I (as CEO) must do':

1. Develop a personal Vision - what do I want to accomplish in my life?

2. Tell the truth about current reality.

3. Do the tough things no one else wants to do.

4. Restructure the Top TEAM, if necessary.

5. Build a powerful guiding coalition — management and board.

6. Guide the creation of a shared VISION.

7. Take the responsibility of being the main change agent.

8. Create endless opportunities for two-way communications.

9. Create opportunities for Innovations in the rank and file.

10. Maintain Focus.

11. Realign HR Systems; overcome obstacles.

12. Model the desired managerial behaviour - above all maintain CREDIBILITY.

13. Preserve the core values of Tatas (*and my own*). [3a]

Dr. Irani presented a small memento to every senior officer of the company with the following quote inscribed on it:

"Vision without action is merely a dream,

Action without vision just passes the time,

Vision with action can change the world."

— *Joel Arthur Barker*

Execution Excellence cannot occur without bias for action!

A TRUE LEADER ALWAYS LEADS BY EXAMPLE

During my years at Tata Steel, I had regular meetings with Dr. Irani. In one of them, sometime in late-1989, I mentioned to him that I was going to write a book on Value Engineering. When he heard that there was not a single book on Value Engineering with Indian case studies, he said, *"Oh, that's a great idea. I would encourage you to do that. And if you are writing a book, it would be better for you to understand how to go about doing it. Meet Dr. Amit Chatterjee. Tell him that I have asked you to meet him."* Dr. Amit Chatterjee was his advisor and the head of R&D. *"Of course, I will do that, Sir,"* was my instant reply.

I called Dr. Amit Chatterjee and told him the context. He said, *"You are most welcome."* We fixed up an appointment, and I went to his office to meet him. He was very loving and heard all my ideas and said, *"It would be good for you to start as soon as possible."* He also recommended that I get in touch with some book publishers. He suggested that it would be good to talk to people from Tata McGraw-Hill and gave me a lead to the head in Delhi. As I was leaving his room he said, *"Do you have a computer or a laptop with you?"* I replied, *"No, I don't have either."* He said, *"It would be a good idea to start writing the book using a laptop. It would be helpful as it would ease revisions and editing."* I thanked him for all the suggestions and went back to my room to start my work.

Later I contacted Tata McGraw-Hill to understand how to write the book in detail. They also suggested using a laptop for preparing the script. I was wondering how to get the laptop.

Angel luck was on my side. Two days after my initial discussion with Tata McGraw-Hill, I met Dr. Irani in the office corridors as he was coming down the staircase from his room. I wished him *"Good morning."* He looked at me, smiled, and said, *"Jaggu, you mentioned to me you were writing a book. Did you meet Amit?"* I then briefed him on all that had happened, and I said, *"Dr. Amit Chatterjee had recommended that I have a laptop."* He asked, *"Don't you have one?"* I replied, *"No, Sir, I don't have one."* In the late 1980s, laptops were not a standard feature on every desk of a senior manager, and especially not in a steel plant. He said, *"I see."* He continued down the staircase, probably on his way to another meeting.

In the same afternoon, I got a call from Krishna Rao, who was the Executive Officer to Dr. Irani.

He said, *"Jaggu, could you please come to my office? I have something for you."* I said, *"Sure."*

When I reached his office, a surprise was waiting for me. *"Jaggu, the boss has sanctioned a laptop. You can contact the Management Services Division and get one from them. I'm sending a letter to the Divisional Manager of Management Services."*

I couldn't believe it. Here was a boss who was so understanding and so keen on encouraging his people, and he understood the importance of one of his managers writing a book. More than anything else, he made sure that he provided me with all the assistance for publishing the book.

I had no reason to delay the project, and the book titled *'Getting More at Less Cost – The Value Engineering Way'* was released in 1991 by Dr. Irani at the Indian Value Engineering Society's Eastern Zonal Conference held at Kolkata.

REALISE YOUR POTENTIAL

While in Tata Consultancy Services as CEO, Chandra had initiated a novel programme titled 'Realise Your Potential' with great success. Following simple, disciplined approaches, associates of Tata Consultancy Services could achieve extraordinary results. Associates used the opportunities to excel in various activities, outside of the regular office hours, provided by the company, including yoga trainers, marathon running, music, and many more. Chandra demonstrated this through his own example. He has run several marathons including those in Amsterdam, Boston, Chicago, Berlin, Mumbai, New York, and Tokyo. He is an example, a role model for hard work, clear focus, and strategic thinking. No wonder his successor Rajesh Gopinathan, the current CEO of Tata Consultancy Services, continues to achieve extraordinary results following the footsteps of his boss. Actions speak volumes.

"What you do has a far greater impact than what you say."

— *Stephen Covey*

TAKEAWAYS

1. Accomplishing the set goals is a top priority for great leaders.
2. Great leaders boldly and clearly communicate through their actions.
3. Organisational processes should be designed to demand quick action.
4. Actions demonstrate commitment as in the acronym below:

   Accomplishment.

   Communication.

   Task clarity.

   Information validity.

   Organisation culture, and

   Never give up attitude.
5. Great leaders' actions influence the organisational culture.

REFLECTIONS

1. How often have I procrastinated about decision making without valid reasons?
2. Am I clear about my personal goal(s) in life? Do I take action to achieve those goals?
3. In personal and professional life, do I practise before I preach?
4. Do I validate the information before I use it?

He who
can no longer
pause to wonder
and stand
rapt in awe,
is as good as dead;
his eyes are closed.

— *Albert Einstein*

4 THE VIRTUE OF RESPECT

My awe indeed is respect

T he word 'respect' comes from the Latin word *'respectus'* meaning attention, regard or consideration. Great leaders, whom I would like to call 'HEART Leaders' show respect very naturally, and without any compulsion. Usually, respect is associated with courtesy and the regard shown to people. But I have known leaders who have not only respect for people but also genuine respect for rules and regulations, ethics, society, environment, commitment, and time. Let us discuss.

ANCIENT WISDOM

It is an ancient Indian tradition to show respect to one's parents, teachers, and guests, as they are considered embodiments of Divinity.

मातृ देवो भव।	*Maathru Devo Bhava*	*Respect thy Mother as God.*
पितृ देवो भव।	*Pithru Devo Bhava*	*Respect thy Father as God.*
आचार्य देवो भव।	*Aacharya Devo Bhava*	*Respect thy Teacher as God.*
अतिथि देवो भव॥	*Athidhi Devo Bhava.*	*Respect thy Guest as God.*

These verses are from the Taittiriya Upanishad, one of the ten major Upanishads of Vedic literature. The Vedas, the most ancient scriptural texts known to humanity, declare that all that exists is Brahman, the Supreme Divinity. They underscore the need for a vision that considers all beings equal, and to respect all beings as embodiments of the One Divine Principle. Indian culture teaches that all living and non-living things must be respected, loved, and worshipped. No wonder Indian scriptures are replete with stories and anecdotes that reflect the worship of mountains, rivers, forests, trees, and animals. Then why not respect and treat with esteem, and honour the best creation on this earth – human beings? Love and respect for others form the credo of almost all faiths across the world.

RESPECT FOR PEOPLE

A study of HEART Leaders across centuries reveals that interacting with all people with respect comes to them naturally. All of them, without exception, showed great respect for people.

Gandhi is well known for his fair and equal treatment of people of all castes, races, religions, and colours. Mother Teresa saw Jesus in the people who were homeless and abandoned on the streets of Kolkata. As a Scientist, Dr. APJ Abdul Kalam put his colleagues first, and then himself when it came to sharing the limelight.

I would like to share an actual incident that happened in my life.

DISRESPECT IS SURE TO BOOMERANG

On the contrary, leaders who disrespected their team members, the people of the community, and human beings at large, in return get treated with disregard, disgust, and disrespect. However, one benefit I did notice from such leaders' behaviour is that they clearly showed us what a good leader should not do.

I was truly fortunate that in the forty-plus years of my corporate career, I came across just two such leaders. I had a senior colleague, Joe Fernandes (name changed), who joined as the Vice President and Head of Manufacturing, Supply-chain, HR, and Administration. I had known Joe for some time, through industry association meetings, even before he joined our division as VP. But my perception of him completely changed when I saw him from close quarters.

Right from day one, he showed his true colours. I am sure he never heard the actor Meryl Streep, recognised with the most prestigious awards of her industry, say, *"Disrespect invites disrespect."*

Joe used to take a walk with all of his direct reports and told us that he was practising Management By Wandering Around (MBWA)! One day he found some water spilt on the floor and shouted at the Head of HR to get a cloth and clean the floor.

The event I am describing happened in front of some shop floor associates. The HR head, who was a gentle and notably well-behaved person, did not want a scene, and quietly picked up the nearby cloth and started to wipe the floor. Another day, during a MBWA moment with Joe, the Head of Administration fell victim to one of his acts.

I couldn't stand by anymore and accept his bullying behaviour. When the round was over, I sought time with him and met him in his office. I politely explained the concerns of his direct reports. He looked at me sternly and said, *"That's my style. As a boss I know how to get things done,"* and turned his back to make coffee for himself!

That shocked me! I said to myself, "How long will this leadership style of disrespect continue?" The result came after a few months. The top management fired him. For a long time, I wondered how the company had tolerated him for those few months and allowed him to demoralise the entire team.

After about three years, I happened to meet him in Bengaluru airport while waiting for a flight to Chennai. He smiled at me and greeted me warmly. We had a brief but pleasant chat. It appeared to me that he had dropped his ego considerably and changed for the better.

Kiana Tom, the award-winning fitness expert and American TV host once said, *"Treat everyone with respect and kindness. Period. No exceptions."*

I learnt through reading, observations, talks, actions, and interactions with different people, that HEART Leaders showed respect to everyone by following simple actions.

LISTEN WITH UNDIVIDED ATTENTION

In my observations, the HEART Leaders showed a keen interest in others by tuning in altogether. During conversations with them, they maintained eye-to-eye contact and did not hesitate to seek clarifications where required. Generally, distractions were never allowed like phone calls or reading of emails. In short, they did no multi-tasking. Focus on listening is a great way to show respect for others. Here is an example from my own life as I began my professional career.

After my Master's in Industrial Management from the prestigious Indian Institute of Technology (IIT), Madras, I started working for Larsen and Toubro Ltd, India's leading engineering company, in 1972, Bombay, India. I joined the company as a Post Graduate Trainee in the Valves Division of the Regional Sales Office. My area was Sales of Valves manufactured by the company's subsidiary, Audco India Limited, located in Chennai. I was asked to focus on all current and prospective customers in the States of Gujarat and Madhya Pradesh. It was very clear and there was no ambiguity.

One day, I had the privilege of being invited by the Regional Sales Manager S P Goel (SPG) for a meeting. He was a senior executive and a very respected leader in the company. He wanted to know about my work, what I had learnt and how I planned to achieve my targets. It was a very interactive session and he showed keen interest in listening to all that I had to say. Before he started the meeting, he told his secretary that he should not be disturbed for the next thirty minutes. It was really that way - no calls, no papers came in, no one dropped in, no interference at all. That little instruction to the secretary also indirectly signalled to me that I had thirty minutes with him, and I should be brief and to the point.

I started explaining my plans, the way I had classified the customers in my region into three categories: A, B, and C using the Pareto Analysis. This was backed by a strategy to allocate my time with customers, based on the A, B, and C categorisation. I had worked out the potential sales volumes based on important known large expansion projects undertaken by some of the customers. I told him about the customer listening posts I had informally set up with category A customers.

During the time I was talking, SPG kept his attention fully on me and on what I said. Occasionally, he made some notes and sought clarifications on a few points. At the end of our meeting, he beautifully summarised the discussion and appreciated the points and wished me good luck in my endeavour. He added, *"Please do not hesitate to ask for any help if you need it."*

SPG was an example of an extremely good listener. He clearly demonstrated his respect for me, and valued his and my time as well, even though I was just a trainee working for the company.

APPLAUD A GREAT JOB – WHEN YOU SEE IT

The Annual Awards Ceremony at Tata Steel was a great event to watch. Creative methods were applied for novelty and fun. The Value Engineering Awards Night was no exception. Dr. Jamshed Irani, MD had blocked the 26th December as the Value Engineering night. As Managing Director, he awarded, year after year, dozens of successful teams on this Awards Night. The Value Engineering Division set up a process that was meticulously followed. Every team that had completed their projects calculated the cost saved, which was verified by an audit team. Based on their audit certificate, the Value Engineering Division invited the successful teams to the recognition night.

The Value Engineering Awards Night celebrations were the brainchild of Ashok Pandit, a seasoned professional who was my boss at that time. He suggested that we invite award winners' spouses too. The function was attended by approximately 150 senior leaders and their spouses. The award included a certificate of congratulations, signed by the MD, with useful gifts for the spouse like high-end branded kitchen utensils, designer jewellery boxes, candle stands, and general items which the spouse would like to possess but may not be able to afford. Mrs. Daisy Irani, the wife of the MD, selected these gifts, thereby adding an exceptional human touch. In the first year of recognition, only a few teams qualified. However, the news of the award spread across company officials, and the momentum gathered. Several hundred teams started happily participating in the company's Value Engineering Programme.

Tata Steel gained substantially through its strong belief that all employees must be respected and recognised for their success as individuals and through the various teams they were involved in projects such as Value Engineering, Quality Improvements, and Quality Circles. The direct impact was a substantial improvement in the profitability of the company, better value to customers, greater process efficiencies, high team spirit, and improved employee satisfaction. Highlighting and involving family members in the success of employees can play a significant role in not only ensuring a good work-life balance, but also cooperation from home to enhance productivity, and industrial peace. These have a direct and positive impact on the company's performance. It may be noted that Tata Steel holds an international record for having the most cordial and productive relationships with its workforce through effective Industrial Relations and Personnel Management for nearly a century.

APPLAUDING ACHIEVEMENTS OF EMPLOYEE'S FAMILY

One of the toughest entrance exams in the world for admissions to colleges is the All India Joint Entrance Examination (JEE) to the most prestigious IITs. Admissions to the IITs is most sought after by students all over India and even overseas. Approximately a million students appear in the tests and the number of students admitted is around 13,650, which works out to 1.36%! So, when a Tata Steel employee's son Abhinav Kumar achieved the first rank in the All India JEE in 1998 and was selected by MIT for undergraduate studies, Dr. Irani, the Managing Director of the company, recognised the 12th grader in the presence of all the senior officers. As a token of appreciation, he was presented with the best laptop computer available at that time.

PRIVACY MATTERS

HEART Leaders praise and reward their colleagues always in the presence of a large gathering. But when they want to counsel or reprimand someone, they make sure that they do so in private. This respects the individual's self-esteem, helps, and improves understanding and creates a healthy win-win atmosphere. Great leaders accept the fact that every individual is different and have different perceptions and behaviour towards the same or similar situations. As Mahatma Gandhi said, *"Honest differences are often a healthy sign of progress."*

Other ways of showing respect include saying thank you or doing simple acts like walking to the door with the guest or opening the door of the car for others. Such simple respectful acts do not in any way lower their self-esteem but result in healthy interactions and builds lasting relationships. Some say actions speak louder than words. Yet we know that one cannot fake for long and will not be able to put on an act of these small gestures for a long time — unless it turns into a habit and one finds joy in these small acts of kindness.

ENVIRONMENT, SOCIETY, AND GOVERNANCE

The World Economic Forum that met in January 2020 at Davos, Switzerland, emphasised Stakeholder Capitalism. The participating corporate leaders stressed the importance of Environmental, Social, and Governance (ESG) parameters during strategy formulation and decision making. The Big Four accounting firms were engaged by WEF to suggest metrics for measuring ESG performance of corporations. The panellists included chairpersons from Bank of America, Siemens, IBM, Salesforce.com, and Royal DSM NV. They reiterated the point that in the long-term it is imperative that CEOs and other business leaders should sign and support the cause of ESG. In another panel discussion Satya Nadella, now Chairman of Microsoft Inc., even agreed to link executive compensation to ESG metrics.

In contrast, the Tata Group's top leadership has paid great attention to ESG right from the beginning, when the group was founded by Jamsetji Tata in 1868. At the age of thirty-five, he established Empress Mills (in 1874), at Nagpur, India. He was such a visionary leader that what we are discussing in 2020, he envisioned and implemented in the late 1800s. He introduced several labour welfare measures in his companies which even industrialised nations from the West did not have at that time. A Provident Fund Scheme was introduced in 1886, a pension fund in 1887, and an accident compensation scheme in 1895. He held a prize day, annually, where thousands of workers participated, dressed in colourful holiday attire. The prizes included gold and silver watches and chains, armlets, medals, and bundles of cloth.

At the opening of the extension of Empress Mills in 1895, Jamsetji said, *"We do not claim to be more unselfish, more generous, or more philanthropic than other people. But, we think, we started on sound and straightforward business principles, considering the interests of our shareholders our own, and the health and welfare of our employees the sure foundation of our prosperity."* [4a]

THE STEEL CITY

In a letter to his son, Dorab Tata, in 1902, Jamsetji shared his vision about the future steel city that his group would build. He wrote:

> *"Be sure to lay wide streets planted with shady trees, every other of a quick-growing variety. Be sure that there is plenty of space for lawns and gardens. Reserve large areas for football, hockey and parks ... "* [4b]

Though Jamsetji did not live to see the beautiful city, his dream for a green city has been well kept by successive leadership teams for over a century. The city of Jamshedpur, known as the steel city, is acknowledged for its greenery, especially the beautiful Gulmohar trees that line the side of clean wide roads. The Tata Steel Plant boasts of a rose garden, inside the steel plant, adjacent to the General Manager's (Works) office, and in front of the battery of coke ovens! Migratory birds have even been spotted here!

Acknowledging the vital role of ecological conservation as part of the larger corporate mandate. Tata group chairman JRD Tata had once said, *"We did not have to create a lake to produce a truck. But we did."* [4b] This is the kind of visionary commitment to ESG that subsequent generations of the Tata Group leaders have displayed.

RULES AND REGULATIONS

HEART Leaders adhere to the laws of the state. JRD Tata is known for his adherence to high ethical standards of governance. His passion for flying resulted in the founding of Tata Airlines, the first commercial airline company in 1932. The international operations commenced with the inaugural flight from Bombay to London on the 8th June 1948.

In his letter dated the 24th June 1971, addressed to MAS Dalal, one of the officers of Air-India, he wrote, *"I received a parcel of bandages sent, through you, by Lord Harewood for some friend of his in Madras. I was upset at this breach of the Airline's regulations in which I was made to be involved. In future, please do not hesitate to turn down such requests from anybody. If anything is sent to me, it should be sent properly documented and through the customs."*[4b]

Tax consultants were hired by many rich and almost all companies to correctly interpret the ever-changing tax laws to differentiate between what part of income or earnings was lawfully taxable, and what part was avoidable. Tax consultants specialised in advising clients on 'how to avoid paying taxes.' In a way, it meant tax evasion. JRD Tata had his own interpretation based on moral and ethical grounds. One of India's best-known tax consultants, Dinesh Vyas, once shared that JRD never entered a debate between 'tax avoidance' which was permissible, and 'tax evasion' which was illegal. His sole motto was 'tax compliance'. On one occasion, a senior executive of a Tata Company tried to save taxes. Before putting up the case, the chairman of that company took him along to JRD. Dinesh Vyas explained to JRD:

"But Sir, it is not illegal."

Softly, JRD replied, "Not illegal, yes. But is it right?"

Vyas had said that never in his decades of professional work had anyone asked him that question. He later wrote in an article, *"JRD would have been the most ardent supporter of the view expressed by Lord Denning, 'The avoidance of tax may be lawful, but it is not yet a virtue.'"* [4c] Both these anecdotes are indicative of the high standards of governance practised by the Group Chairman of India's largest conglomerate more than 60-70 years ago. His decisions underscored that Business and Ethics aren't oxymorons.

PROMISES TO BE KEPT

There is a famous saying in Ramayana, the Indian epic which describes the great rulers of the Raghu dynasty. *'Raghu Kula Reeti Sada Chali Aayi, Prana Jaaye Par Vachan Na Jaaye.'* Translated into English it means that it was the tradition of the rulers of the Raghu clan that they would keep their promises even at the cost of their own lives. To fulfil the promise his father, King Dasharatha, made to his Queen Kaikeya, Rama (his son from Queen Kaushalya) happily accepted an exile to the forests for fourteen years.

WHAT ABOUT IN THE CORPORATE WORLD?

Jamsetji Tata's adherence to an ethical management style was sacrosanct. The principles of honesty, humility, excellence, respect for people, and the welfare of the society laid down by him were strictly adhered to by every successor at the Tata Group. After India's political independence in 1947, businesses came under several rules and regulations as part of the first Prime Minister – Jawaharlal Nehru's passion for socialism and centralised planning as the means for growth and development. At that time, companies needed to take approvals from numerous government agencies to set up a business legally. Manufacturing, in particular, was heavily regulated. Licences were required for starting new companies, for producing new products, and even for expanding production capacities.

This led to red tape and corruption. Business growth through unfair means was the rule of the day. The 'License Raj' as it was called, (administration through licenses) was an outcome of the government industrial licensing policy. The License Raj that showed initial success in the 1950s eventually led to low rates of growth and investment. However, this system continued for nearly 45 years as his daughter, Indira Gandhi, who succeeded him as India's third Prime Minister, imposed even more stringent laws and unprecedented levels of taxation. The highest bracket was 95% taxation. India began to liberalise its economy only in the early 1990s, ending the License Raj under Prime Minister PV Narasimha Rao.

In the 1960s and 1970s, Tatas were not growing as much as some other industrial groups did. All major projects including a car manufacturing plant were disallowed by the government. Under the License Raj, the Tata Group suffered its legitimate growth because the top leadership wanted growth only by following fair means. On this matter, in a conversation with RM Lala, the author who wrote several books on Tatas, JRD says, *"We feel a certain pride that we are somewhat different from others. This factor has also worked against our growth. What would have happened if our philosophy was like that of some other companies which do not stop at any means to attain their ends? I have often thought of that, and I have concluded that if we were like these other groups, we would be twice as big as we are today. What we have sacrificed is 100 percent growth. But we wouldn't want it any other way."* [4d]

Globally, we see politicians make commitments and promise a glorious future for the people, state, and the country. The actual results are far from the picture they paint. However, we do have public figures who make commitments and stick by them. Here is an example from the 21st century.

In 2009, First Lady Michelle Obama made a commitment. She saw the urgent need for dealing with the growing problem of childhood obesity in the USA. She launched a major initiative *'Let's Move!'* and committed her services to this national cause. She persuaded the business houses from the food industry to support the cause. Voluntarily many came forward and made commitments. Since the obesity challenge was of a long-term nature, the need was felt for an organisation at the national level that could mitigate the growing challenge. To meet these needs, the Partnership for a Healthier America (PHA) was created.

During the last ten years, this organisation has done pioneering work on several fronts, including winning commitments from industries, working in the areas of increasing physical activity, shaping early palates, shifting retail environments, and healthier school campuses.

Michelle once observed, *"If I made a commitment, I stood by that commitment – and try to make it real. Because when you become leaders, the most important thing you have is your word, your trust. That's where respect comes from."*

RESPECT FOR TIME

HEART Leaders always respect their time and that of others. A common quality with them is punctuality. When I joined the Visvesvaraya National Institute of Technology in Nagpur, in 1965, I heard from my civil engineering professor about the great technocrat in whose honour the institution was named. Sir Mokshagundam Visvesvaraya was a civil engineer par excellence. He was a recipient of India's highest civilian honour, the Bharat Ratna, in 1955. His birth date the 15th September is celebrated as 'Engineers' Day', all over India. He is known as the builder of modern India. A great patriot, he dedicated his efforts to the upliftment of his countrymen. Realising the need for self-sufficiency, he gave the slogan, 'Industrialise or Perish'. While in my second year of engineering, I was preparing for a speech to be delivered on Engineer's Day. To make the talk interesting, I approached the head of the Department of Civil Engineering, Dr. Mokashi, for anecdotes related to Sir Visvesvaraya. He gave me a few and here is one which shows how much he respected the value of time. Dr. Mokashi recounted:

Once a reporter asked Sir Visvesavaraya what he values most? He said: "My country, time, and Civil Engineering!" His punctuality was of an exceedingly high order. He preferred to reach the appointed place five minutes before time and wait in the car rather than go even a minute late. His planning was meticulous and followed a military discipline.[4e]

Mahatma Gandhi is known for his disciplined time management. He had time for meditation, reading various books, writing articles, going for long walks, meeting world leaders, attending sick animals, and learning Tamil from my great grand uncle R. Shankaran Iyer!

On the lighter side, I came across a Strategic Business Unit (SBU) Head who found it very hard to value time. I was conducting a special training programme on Time Management for his SBU, and he readily signed up for the programme. Twenty of his senior managers, including his six direct reports, attended the programme. But the SBU Head was absent. After completing the programme successfully, I met him in his room. He apologised profusely and said, *"I found absolutely no time to attend the Time Management Programme today."* This is not uncommon. They simply do not value their own time.

We also see chronic latecomers for meetings. To deal with all those who came in late, in Tata Consultancy Services, a contribution of $5 for every minute of the delay was collected and used for some charitable cause. Sometimes the amount collected exceeded $100! A similar practice existed in Tata Motors when participants arrived late for training programmes conducted by the Management Training Center.

In 1986, one of my colleagues, Suresh Apte (name changed), was deputed to Japan to study the extent of automation. He had travelled overseas several times and was familiar with what to expect while in a foreign country. He had an appointment with the General Manager of a robotic systems company that specialised in automatic welding equipment. He was advised to catch a local train at 2:04 PM from a particular station and get off at the destination. The train ride was supposed to be for about 43 minutes. He reached the correct station and arrived at the right platform but two minutes late. He saw a train arrive and he dashed in and managed a seat next to a window. He started reading his visit notes. He was going over his discussion points carefully so that he could elicit maximum information in the shortest time. After about 35 minutes he closed his briefcase and was preparing to arrive at the destination. But the train did not stop after 43 minutes and continued non-stop for another 8 minutes. Suresh realised there was something wrong. On enquiry, he realised that he was travelling on a different train and to a different destination. A two minutes delay, at the starting station, caused more than 135 minutes delay with an unwanted embarrassment!

Respect for time is a virtue and is in the DNA of all great leaders. They value their own time and that of others.

TAKEAWAYS

Great leaders show their respect for:

1. **R**ules and regulations of the country.
2. **E**nvironment that balances our ecosystems.
3. **S**ociety we live in.
4. **P**eople we deal with.
5. **E**thical Governance.
6. **C**ommitments we make.
7. **T**ime of self and everyone around them.

REFLECTIONS

1. How often have I broken the rules of the company, city, state, and the country I live in to achieve my personal goal(s)?

2. Do I really care for the environment and the impact of climate change? What steps have I taken to mitigate resource wastage in my home and work area?

3. Am I punctual for all meetings, programmes, and assignment completion?

4. Do I respect people irrespective of their position, colour, gender, education, nationality, religion, language, and age?

5. How often have I spoken ill of others without knowing facts? How many times have I tolerated differences of opinion with others and not felt agitated with them?

6. How often have I recognised or praised a colleague's achievements in life in the presence of others?

Teamwork makes
the dream work,
but a vision
becomes a nightmare
when the leader
 has a big dream
and a bad team.

— *John C. Maxwell*

5 TEAMS@WORK

I saw human factors in the greatest teamwork

In the HEART Leadership, we discussed the qualities of Humility, Excellence, Action, and Respect. Each one of them is vital to make a good leader into a great leader. However, even a great leader cannot achieve their goals without the help of a Team. They achieve their goals by selecting and forming great teams. Every member of the team has certain common characteristics. They also need to possess some unique traits. It is the great leaders' challenge to ensure the proper blend to attain high performance. The string that connects the pearls of Humility, Action, and Respect, as a precondition for Excellence is Teamwork. A group of people showered with wisdom, humility, and a deep appreciation for one another can create an action ground for teamwork to successfully play.

LEARNING FROM THE CULINARY ART

My wife Lalitha is an expert in culinary art. She delights in trying out different dishes from various vegetarian cuisines. Every time, the dishes come out delicious and our guests enjoy whatever she cooks. When I tried the same recipes independently, they barely managed to qualify as being edible! She always told me that you need to add all the ingredients in the correct proportions to get the best flavour to satisfy the taste buds of most guests. Her favourite example is the *'eggless walnut and date cake.'* She says, *"Just because I like dates, I do not add 12 dates instead of the 8 suggested in the recipe or add rose essence instead of vanilla essence! Every ingredient has a unique quality and adds a special flavour to the item being cooked. Even though every constituent has its own flavour, when they are mixed in the right proportions, and cooked for the required time, and at the correct temperature and pressure, the flavours blend well and give the dish the taste that makes it special! Most importantly never ever forget to include a large portion of love throughout the cooking process."* That is the secret to great recipes from a seasoned chef!

That triggered my thinking machine. Watching an old episode of *'The Iron Chef America',* a thought flashed across my mind. What if the great leaders were made to prepare a recipe for a high performing team? I researched large and small teams that have effectively performed and achieved their goals, and the way great leaders built their teams for success. Directly or indirectly all high performing teams showed several common traits.

For example, an aircrew remains as one team just for the duration of the flight. The captain, co-pilot, purser, and flight attendants may be meeting for the first time just before the flight. Yet they have the highest responsibility of making sure that all passengers are taken to their destination safely. But the aircrew is part of a larger team of staff responsible for ticketing, check-in, baggage, maintenance, meteorology, air traffic control, security, hygiene, airport management, and the list continues! The success of the aircrew lies in understanding clearly the most important common highest goal:

the safety of all passengers. Complete knowledge of their duties and responsibilities, respect for other members of the team, willingness to sacrifice their own comfort for others, a positive attitude, creativity to seek alternate solutions, remaining cool under emergency conditions, good communication, humility to learn from others, and a great sense of humour, are some of the ingredients that I observed with some of the best airlines crew.

Many of us have enjoyed the sense of humour of the Southwest Airlines staff, the way they welcome us and educate us on safety rules. Announcements on safety rules are very important to all passengers but when they are delivered in a monotonous tone and drab manner this turns off the passenger. Whereas when presented in a jovial, and enthusiastic manner this arouses the interest of all passengers.

A MIRACLE ON THE HUDSON

It was a Thursday. I was very busy with my preparation for a business presentation in my office in Santa Clara when my friend Alex called me from Jersey City. He sounded excited and concerned at the same time. *"Jaggu, an Airbus 320 has crashed into the Hudson River in New York. Turn on the TV."* Before I could ask for more information, he was gone. I had no TV nearby, and so I called my wife, who was my most reliable source of information, but she drew a blank as she was busy with her work. She promised to update me with the latest news.

I wonder what happened on the 15th January 2009.

US Airways Flight 1549 took off from LaGuardia Airport at 3:26 bound for Charlotte, North Carolina. It was a normal takeoff with 155 passengers on board. Captain Chesley Sullenberger was in command. After about three minutes of being airborne, both engines lost thrust following a collision with a flock of geese at a low altitude. Captain Chesley took a decision, in almost a split second, and landed the Airbus A320-214 in New York's freezing Hudson River, saving all 155 passengers and crew on board. A truly chilling experience for everyone knowing that on the 15th January the Hudson's temperature was recorded at 6°F below zero. It was a miracle on the Hudson! Appreciation was poured on Captain Chesley Sullenberger for the creative way he landed the plane. We know how difficult the situation must have been. The entire crew did a marvellous job and deserved appreciation. The entire team rose together, as one, performed all needed tasks, and delivered excellently what they were expected to do – ensuring the safety of all passengers, even in that extraordinary situation.

Similarly, a team of surgeons, doctors, anesthesiologists, and other technicians who get together, probably a few hours before an operation, as a team, perform their duties with diligence, discipline, and dedication to complete their task of relieving pain or saving a human life. The exemplary role played by the team of medical practitioners, technicians, scientists, and staff to address the current pandemic is an example of chivalry, dedication, and selfless service rendered to the entire humanity.

Sports teams like basketball, soccer, and hockey teams, although they remain as one team for the duration of the game, invariably have the advantage of knowing each other beforehand during the practice sessions. Almost all traits mentioned for the aircrew is applicable to the team of doctors, and the sports teams as well.

QUICK ACTION TEAMS FOR EMERGENCY

Rewind the clock sixteen years, to that unforgettable and dreadful Monday 29th August 2005. The ferocious hurricane Katrina struck the sleepy residents of New Orleans, Louisiana, who woke up in agony to face one of the worst calamities.

This was the worst natural disaster in American history and cost more than $100 billion in damages. By nightfall, about 75-80% of the city's population had been evacuated.

The city and the surroundings lost communication and electrical power lines. In that chaotic situation about 20,000 stranded citizens gathered at the New Orleans Superdome with great difficulty. Many took shelter at an overpass on Interstate 10 and others at the Ernest N. Morial Convention Center.

They had nothing with them except their lives and probably a backpack with a few essentials they thought may be required. Some of the displaced were so unfortunate that they had seen their homes being brought down to the ground, uprooted by the powerful hurricane and broken like biscuits.

By nightfall, more than 80% of the city was flooded. Water, water everywhere, but no water to drink. The situation was grim.

People became desperate for food and water and the civic amenities had broken down.

Under these circumstances, it was Walmart, the leader in the business world that recognised the poignant situation and stepped in. The emergency team they assembled with such precise communication, powerful conviction, and perfect commitment is praiseworthy. The Chief Executive Officer of Walmart, Lee Scott, on hearing about the mountainous damage caused by Katrina, issued a simple edict, *"This company will respond to the level of this disaster,"* he was remembered to have said in a meeting with his senior management. *"A lot of you are going to have to make decisions above your level. Make the best decision that you can with the information that's available to you at the time, and, above all, do the right thing."*

As one of the officers at the meeting later recalled, *"That was it."* The edict was passed down to store managers and set the tone for how people were expected to react. On the most immediate level, Walmart had 126 stores closed due to damage and power outages. Twenty thousand employees and their family members were displaced. The initial focus was on helping them. And within forty-eight hours, more than half of the damaged stores were up and running again. But according to one executive on the scene, as word of the disaster's impact on the city's population began filtering in from Walmart employees on the ground, the priority shifted from reopening stores to, *"Oh, my God, what can we do to help these people?"* Acting on their own authority, Walmart's store managers began distributing diapers, water, baby formula, and ice to residents. [5a]

The full relief and recovery took months of struggle and involved several dozen different functional teams. The emergency help and service provided by the Walmart managers show us excellent Teamwork, motivated by great leadership. Positive attitude, willingness to sacrifice, timely action, empowerment, excellent communication, commitment to serve, and respect for people was evident in their teamwork.

MT. SHERMAN, COLORADO

Let's shift gears. What about the teams that climb snowclad mountain peaks? Let me share one of my experiences as I happened to be a member of one such team. It is easy to discuss the qualities required for a team to succeed in a classroom situation. However, it is a different ball game to engage the team, and expect the members to show positive attitudes, willingness to make sacrifices, and show respect for fellow members while doing the task. The team is the field where these qualities are tested and tried out for success. The team should not only have these quality ingredients in the right proportions but should be blended well by the team leader. We saw that in the example of Walmart's CEO taking the great leader's role by addressing and alleviating the problems faced by fellow human beings during the Katrina disaster. The principle behind every successful team is almost the same: starts with a great leader.

Given the goal to be achieved, the great leader decides his/her priorities. For example, I was part of a team of 22 executives of Tata Technologies who were attending a three-day Leadership Meet in Denver, Colorado, USA. The CEO, Pat McGoldrick and the Chief

Operating Officer, Warren Harris came up with the idea that as part of a Team Building exercise, all of us should undertake a trek to reach the 14,100 feet summit of Mount Sherman. All of us were informed well in advance so that we had time to prepare ourselves for the adventure trek on the snowy mountain.

For most of us, it was the first time climbing a snowclad mountain. As a college student, the highest peak I had climbed was Jaku Hills, approximately 9,000 feet high, near Shimla in Himachal Pradesh, India. That was almost 40 years earlier! The conditions were completely different. I was 17 then and the trek was on well-paved roads with no snow!

One of our colleagues Kevin Noe, Chief of Marketing, who had climbed several mountain peaks, 20,000 feet and above, across all of the continents was the best choice as the leader. He set the rules right in the beginning. Good leaders know how to take care of all requirements through their study of the subject, discussions with experts and their own experience. When Kevin learnt that there were two people, including me, who were about 60 years in age, and others were in their mid-thirties and early fifties, he decided that there should be at least two additional members in the team who had the requisite experience and could become our buddies during the trek. Since there was no one from our organisation who satisfied this experience requirement, two of Kevin's mountaineering friends were asked to join us in this adventure as our buddies/guides.

From the day the announcements were made, he started communicating and explained patiently about the trek. We had several online meetings to discuss what we should do: the type of exercises to practise; how to get acclimatised to the environment; the kind of special gear and shoes to wear; medical kits and water bottles to carry, and many other points. No minor details were left out. He patiently answered all questions to the fullest satisfaction of the team. He also cautioned on what we should not do before, during and after the trek. Most importantly, I think he invested his time wisely in motivating all of us and gave positive assurances to all of us that *"we can do it"*.

We were divided into smaller clusters of four or five people, depending on our ability to move fast or slow. A day before the actual trek we had a practise session at our base camp at approximately 12,000 feet ASL. We learnt the importance of being in small teams, the need for hydrating ourselves, and how to manage slippery conditions.

The next day, with a powerful motivational speech, Kevin drove so much enthusiasm that even the most sceptical amongst us decided to accept the challenge and complete the ascent. He handed over our branded caps, a packet of high energy snacks, and two bottles of water. He said *"smile"* and clicked a photograph with all of us posing with our thumbs up!

On the way up, there were several challenging moments. Every time I experienced difficulty, the buddy expert was available to help. Kevin kept motivating each one of us. He moved from one cluster to another to make sure everyone was feeling good. When we reached the summit, after a gruelling climb of approximately two and a half hours, all the clusters that were ahead of us were waiting patiently with great humility to allow the two most senior (*in age*) the opportunity to reach the peak first, in recognition of our ability to undertake the trek despite our ages. The leader, Kevon Noe, stood aside and was busy taking photographs of the successful climbers.

Although Kevin had some family commitments almost at the same time, he sacrificed his personal time, self-interest, credit, and the spotlight to make sure we succeeded. He led 22 novices to success in mountaineering, which is very demanding. A great job indeed. A great leader gets extraordinary results from ordinary people!

CRICKET AND SACRIFICE?

As a lover of cricket, how can I ignore this team sport? Cricket and cricketers are known for making millions of dollars in every season they play. The more success they achieve, the more money they receive the next season. However, here too there are some outstanding players of high character who stand out as exemplary. They sacrificed their personal success for the sake of the game. This makes the players not only better as cricketers but as human beings. Over so many years, cricket has seen a lot of history being created on and off the field. Here are some excerpts that capture the best moments that could touch any person's heart.

Gautam Gambhir and Virat Kohli, two Delhi batsmen shared a very touching moment when the former decided to sacrifice his prize in order to respect the latter's efforts. When India had to chase a mammoth 315 runs in the Eden Gardens, Kolkata (2009) against

Sri Lanka, Gambhir and Kohli stitched a match-winning 224 run partnership to help their country cross the line safely. Kohli scored his first century during the chase and was then out for 107. However, Gambhir remained unbeaten on 150 and ensured victory. When the Man of the Match Award was given to Gambhir, he passed it on to Kohli as an appreciation of the youngster's efforts. This act of selflessness touched many fans and projected the kinder side of Gambhir.

Adam Gilchrist is probably the best wicketkeeper-batsman world cricket has ever seen. His ability to turn match results with the bat and not leave a single opportunity to stump the batsman is something that defines his career. However, the Australian wicketkeeper was not only the best player the team had but also the best opponent other teams could hope for. Players sacrifice for their team, but Adam demonstrated kindness for the opponent.

It was the World Cup semi-final match and Australia was playing Sri Lanka. The kangaroos started well by reaching a score of 34-0 in just 5 overs. Winning the world cup wouldn't have gained '*Gilly*' as much fame as his actions at the end of the 5th over did. Gilchrist tried to sweep Aravinda de Silva but managed only an edge that the umpire failed to notice. The Sri Lankans stood surprised and disappointed before Adam Gilchrist walked off the pitch. The entire cricket fraternity was surprised to see such respect for the game. Gilchrist is always remembered for his ethics and this act carved his name on the moral wall of cricket. [5b]

A CAPTAIN WHO IS A TEAM PLAYER

As captain of the Indian cricket team, Sourav Ganguly, is also known to be a first-rate manager too. He encourages teammates both on and off the field. Sourav said: *"At any time, there will be somebody playing outstandingly, somebody struggling, and it is the job of the captain to talk with the guy who's not doing well and make sure he feels good."* [5c]

No wonder that Sourav's boss – Tata Steel's Managing Director B. Muthuraman (now retired), maintains that, *"Sourav has demonstrated how to build and manage a team ... how to motivate and convert individuals into a team."* [5c]

The speciality of a sports team is the sacrifice that some members make for the team to win. Rather than seek individual success, they care and feel satisfied with their team's glory.

Basketball is an amazing sport, but selfish play is terrible to watch. Playing on a basketball team where everyone is out for him or herself is sheer misery. Sacrifice is a key element for teams that win. A great player will sacrifice a shot because a teammate is in a better position. A great leader will sacrifice his own glory if it helps the team win. The good news is that when a leader sacrifices for the team, he eventually will get noticed and valued more than if he only thought selfishly. [5d]

There are hundreds of examples of army officers and soldiers trying to save their fellowmen during a battle and sacrificing themselves in the process. The recent Covid-19 pandemic clearly highlighted the sacrifice made by healthcare professionals across the world. Thousands of volunteers belonging to different service organizations conducted themselves commendably and performed yeomen service.

I would like to share another example of a very large team, which, was formed almost in an instance. Various organisations and people came together for a common cause, and I was a happy person who saw and experienced this large team's performance and benefitted from it.

TOGETHER WE FLY!

A sudden and unprecedented strike by Air Traffic Control (ATC) staff in India on the 11th April 1997, caused terrible disruption to air travel throughout Southeast Asia. For, perhaps, the first time in aviation history, no aircraft - international or domestic - flew over Indian air space for close to 30 hours. The reason was a wildcat strike by air traffic controllers (ATCOs) agitating against the suspension of a colleague who was held responsible for a near-collision over Palam airport in Delhi on the 2nd April. The strike resulted in the cancellation or rescheduling of more than 250 flights, leading to chaos in airports all over India and affecting international flights. I was one of the travellers who was affected by this strike in a positive way!

The Confederation of Indian Industry (CII) had organised a special visit to Singapore to study and understand the Service Quality Excellence across all industries. I was one of the 15 privileged delegates of this study group. This programme was very well organised, and it ended on Friday 11th April 1997. We were to take our flights back to our respective destinations in India the same night. I was bound for Kolkata along with two other members of the delegation.

We left the hotel and came to Changi International Airport and checked in with our bags at the Singapore Airlines (SIA) counter. At the time of check-in, the SIA representative at the counter informed us that there could be some delays because of a sudden strike by the Air Traffic Control Staff in India. *"We are not sure when we can take off. We are depending on getting a clear message from India. Be rest assured that we will keep you informed. We are extremely sorry for the inconvenience,"* he said. We were shocked to hear about the strike and were concerned about the delayed departure.

As per the assurance given by SIA staff, they announced updates about the strike situation, and the possible delay, every 15 minutes. Time was ticking and was now past 8 PM. All passengers bound for Kolkata were requested to assemble in a rectangular cordoned area where dinner was arranged. Every individual was offered a boxed dinner, plate, cutlery, napkins, and a bottle of water. Vegetarian and non-vegetarian tags were clearly marked. There were several SIA staff who moved like bees, attending to all passengers. They made sure all of us were served dinner of our choice with a lot of love and care. The staff too joined us and had dinner. *"Is this also a part of the CII training why we were visiting Singapore?"* the critic in me wondered.

The three of us and a SIA staff member were eating and discussing the possible causes for the ATC strike. During the conversation, we learnt that this staff member was actually the General Manager of Singapore Airlines. He was very casually dressed, amazingly simple, and exhibited high humility. He squatted on the floor and was eating the same food as us. This was quite touching. We heard from him that the entire office staff from the city, even those who were not in departments related to Flight Operations were called immediately from home when it was known that dozens of flights were likely to be cancelled. He also said that arrangements were being made for our rest and sleep as well.

Once the dinner was over, we were given blankets, pillows, and bedsheets. He said, *"We are trying to accommodate every one of you in a hotel but please give us some time as we have to find more than 8,000 rooms in the city during a peak weekend. In the meantime, stretch your legs and rest here."* In about an hour there was an announcement informing us that our hotels had been booked and the transport was also arranged to take us to the hotel.

We could leave with our hand luggage and personal belongings. I wondered and asked about our checked-in bags, but everyone was told not to worry and to just carry the bags currently with them. The only important thing was our boarding passes. Even our passports would not be checked! So, we left the customs area and immigration and left the airport in reserved buses to our hotels, showing just our boarding passes.

On arrival at the hotel, check-in was even swifter. The only requirement was the boarding pass. The hotel clerk said, *"As soon as your flights are ready, we will let you know. And anyway, please go to your rooms and have a good night's sleep. We will give you a wake-up call at 6:30 AM."*

I slept well and in the morning I woke up with the announcement that breakfast was ready! So, we had our breakfast and at 8 o'clock, the hotel clerk informed us that the buses were ready to take us back to the airport since the flights would take off at 10.00 AM. We all got on the bus to the airport. Again, it was the same procedure, *"Just show the boarding pass".* The check-in was so smooth that we all reached the departure gates in minutes. Soon we were airborne, and arrived in Kolkata after about four hours of flying. All these arrangements were made, not because I was a special guest or was travelling by Business or First Class. I was an ordinary passenger with an Economy Class ticket and all passengers in the Economy Class received the same service.

Now the most important part was how all these arrangements were made just based on the boarding pass. Nowhere I was asked to sign a document or show my passport. The coordination required was tremendous among Singapore Airlines, Airport Authority, Immigration, Customs, Caterers, Transporters, and Hoteliers. All of them had to be clearly communicated to about the reality on the ground and then decide quickly what needed to be done while keeping in mind the common goal of providing comfort and convenience to the passengers. The service quality excellence was evident in every instance. We had an actual demonstration of it, thanks to the Air Traffic Strikes in India! We got to see how the entire Singapore city came together as one team and met the situation.

Later in my career, I had the good fortune to travel across all the continents, with the exception of Antarctica, by many different airlines. I did face delays and cancellations of flights at several major international airports but never saw the service quality excellence that I experienced on the 11th April 1997 in Singapore. This was amazing, and I thought here is an example of excellent teamwork and great leadership that integrates everything we discussed. Humility, Excellence, Action, Respect, and Teamwork.

Let's take a mixing bowl and start adding the ingredients for high performing teams. It includes:

A Positive attitude, Bias for action, Creativity, Discipline, Excellence, Empowerment, Goal clarity, Good communication, Humility, Human values, Individual skills and capabilities, Major attention to minor details, Organisational values, Respect for other members, Sacrificing personal success for team success, Sharing credit with all members, Thinking big, Understanding roles and responsibilities, Valuing members' time, Willingness to learn ... and the list can go on and on.

As one can see, a great leader, when he/she builds their team, has the challenge to mix and match these key ingredients in the most optimal manner to achieve the best synergistic effect. When done correctly the results are outstanding.

The secret lies in connecting the dots and identifying the key emerging themes. A good leader usually has many of the ingredients included in his team, but a great leader will ensure that he starts with Humility, Excellence, Action, and Respect as the foundation on which the team is built. The team is like a triangular pyramid. The base is Humility, and the three sides are Excellence, Action, and Respect.

What is inside this prism? It is the 'Heart of the HEART — *the Soul*' and is discussed in the next chapter.

TAKEAWAYS

1. Excellent teamwork is the result of the team leader's ability to clearly:

   i. Define the goal to be achieved.

   ii. Communicate and build good understanding among the team members.

   iii. Illustrate the need to sacrifice personal accomplishments for the sake of the team's success.

   iv. Encourage the right behaviour through personal examples.

2. Great leaders make Humility the foundation for teamwork, the base of a pyramid, with its three sides being Excellence, Action, and Respect for each of the team's members.

REFLECTIONS

1. As a leader, have I shown exemplary behaviour before demanding it from my team members?

2. How often have I placed my personal agenda over that of the team?

3. How often have I backed out after making commitments to the team?

4. As a leader, how often have I taken the responsibility for the failure of the team, and given credit for success to the members of the team?

5. Do I clearly communicate what my expectations are before asking the team to start their task?

You have to grow
from the inside out.

None can teach you,
none can
make you
spiritual.

There is
no other teacher
but your own soul.

— *Swami Vivekananda*

6. IT IS DEEP WITHIN

Becoming aware of one's true self

We saw that to move from a Leader's circle to a Great Leader's circle we need to incorporate into our day-to-day processes the HEART characteristics – Humility, Excellence, Action, Respect, and Teamwork. This higher circle is what I call the HEART Leadership.

Is there anything higher to achieve? *"Yes indeed,"* would be my answer. There is one higher circle for leadership to reach, the highest, the Inspiring Leader's circle. To move from a HEART Leader to becoming an Inspiring Leader calls for one major step. The step of realising our Soul, the Supreme Self. Call it Self-Awareness, Self - Realisation, or Realising the Unity in this diverse universe. Names do not matter.

There are two major limiting factors. The first is our perception; not knowing who we really are. Many think self-awareness or self-analysis is just knowing one's strengths and weaknesses. They limit this awareness to their role in the family, the corporate world, and sometimes in the immediate community around them. They forget their role in the larger context as humans, being part of this diverse universe. While the lower level of self-awareness is agreeable to them, it is not good enough for entering the Inspiring Leader's circle. Socrates, the great Greek philosopher, summarised this matter well when he said, *"The unexamined life is not worth living."* Knowing, *"Who am I?"*, *"What is my purpose in life?"* and *"How do I achieve it?"* helps us to discover our deeper Inner Self.

After all, it's not about what kind of leader one wants to be;
it starts with self-reflection about what kind of person you ought to be.

For example, anything we *'know'* or are *'aware of'* cannot be us! When we say *"this laptop is mine"* we are clearly identifying the laptop as different from ourselves. The laptop becomes the object and we become the subject. We can touch, see, and experience the efficacy of the laptop. What we experience has got to be different from our true 'Self'. Similarly, we are aware of the changes that the body goes through right from the time we are born. Something within us is aware of the changes taking place in our bodies. Thus, the body is the object, and we are the subject. So, we cannot be the body. Similarly, we are aware of our thoughts, decisions, and understanding of science and technology. This again means that we are not the mind and the intellect! We are something subtler, changeless, and deeper within, that is present throughout our lifetime as a witness to the external world (*through the senses*), witness to the changes in the body, the thoughts in the mind, and the nuances of the intellect. Body, mind, and intellect conglomerate are different from our Self. That which is the innermost, self-luminescent principle that we truly are. This is referred to as True Self, True Consciousness, or True Awareness. I call this 'Supreme Self'. This same Self or consciousness is present in all living beings, be it an ant, a butterfly, a peacock, a lion, or humans. Only the level of manifestation differs. When this Awareness of the unity of all creation grows deep within and becomes a living experience, we no longer limit ourselves to this individual body-mind complex. We realise our true Self as being one with all creation, and as the basis of all existence. This is Self-Realisation, also called Nirvana or Liberation.

Across millennia, such a realisation has shown its glimpses in those caring for the environment, not just because the planet is being damaged. At a deeper level, it is about respecting the symbiotic relationship with the environment and the universe — harmony for the greater good.

The second limiting factor is the yardstick used for measuring the level of leadership. On a 4-point scale, 1 being worst, and 4 being most desirable, how do we rate ourselves as leaders? What are the most important measures against which we measure our success as a leader?

Is it shareholder wealth or multi-stakeholder value?

Is it beneficial to us, or does it include the people in the community as well?

Is it profits or success by any means, or only by fair means?

Is it working only for 'me and my family' or does it include care for all beings and the environment we live in?

Is it leading a win-lose game or a win-win game?

Is it happiness and peace for a few or for all?

The deeper the level of Self-Awareness, the higher the level of leadership. From my observations and study of leaders, and great spiritual masters, I have come to identify broadly three levels of awareness in leaders. Leaders who identify with:

Level 1 – I and my.

Level 2 – Community and sometimes country.

Level 3 - All beings in the Universe.

Even within each level, there are several shades. One level does not necessarily represent a single characteristic. Let's analyse these three levels one by one.

Level 1 – I and My: The first is 'The Awareness at the I and My level'. At this level, we observe that leaders' top priority is themselves. All others are considered subservient to them. For this level of leaders what matters is their power, position, possession, publicity, and priorities. They arrogate all success to themselves. One can identify such leaders within minutes as their vocabulary seems to suffer from an overuse of the words 'I' and 'My'. The whole world revolves around the individual and their immediate family. My spouse, my parents, my children, my car, my office, and this continues. Every sentence begins with either 'I' or 'My' . These leaders identify themselves with their body, mind, intellect, and nothing else.

Right from the time we are born, almost all, without exception, associate our name with the body, mind, and intellect we have. We hear phrases like, *"She is strong, beautiful, brilliant,"* or the opposite,

"She is weak, angry, and dull-headed." All these are associated with body, mind, and intellect. We were born into a family and identified with parents and siblings, in relationship to the body. This is a simple and practical way to lead our day-to-day life. There is nothing wrong with this. The problem in identifying with our body, mind, and intellect is that it gives rise to our individuality, and false self-image. The mind of the individual is so powerful that it creates its own world ruled by the mighty emperor — 'The Ego'.

"Ego sees everything as separate; it sees everything as dual. You must remove this ego and see only the Unity. Think only of Unity; think only of the basis of everything." — Sri Sathya Sai Baba

This ego leads to pride and prejudices, likes and dislikes, making life more complicated. We start thinking that our way of doing tasks is the best. When others point out our mistakes, shortcomings, or disagree with our views, opinions, and decisions, we either detest or ignore them. We become happy when our desires are fulfilled and want more of the same. We even nurse additional desires that need to be fulfilled. When they are not satisfied, we are disappointed, sad, and angry. For example, we want to possess the latest BMW and feel thrilled with happiness when we own it. Despite owning a BMW, we become sad with jealousy when we see Jaguars, Ferraris, and Rolls Royces in our neighbourhood! Desire, envy, attachment, anger, greed, and pride are the six devils that engulf and devour us. We become victims of our own false identification, misaligned priorities, and drown ourselves in the ocean of endless sorrow.

If the awareness is at level 1, then the leadership will end up as self-centred, ego-centric, authoritative, and position-driven. The leader would not like to see his position being challenged or his powers being clipped. Any threat to his leadership will be dealt with seriously.

It is not that all leaders at this level of awareness show the same degree of self-centred leadership. There are different shades, gradients in their selfishness. Let me give an analogy. Imagine a tall transparent glass container filled with muddy water. When allowed to settle down, one can see the dark mud at the bottom while the rest of the water is a lighter shade. At the bottom, are the most selfish leaders, willing to use all their wherewithal for satisfying their own ego. They probably don't have an iota of conscience and are willing to cause harm even to their parents and siblings. If they were to be described then words such as inconceivably vicious, merciless, heartless, and inhuman would be used. We could also consider this layer as a thick black line. These different shades of black lines then move towards grey, with the thickness of the lines also gradually thinning. The end of this level could be equivalent to a thin grey line which would mean that this leader could be characterised as selfish and only helping their own family and sycophants who thrive under his/her leadership.

History is replete with examples. Here is an extreme case:

In the Mughal dynasty, Aurangzeb (1618-1707 AD), the third son of Emperor Shah Jahan (1592-1666 AD), killed his own brother Dara Shikoh (1615-1659 AD), the eldest of four brothers, and the rightful heir apparent. Further, he arrested his ailing father Shah Jahan, to occupy the throne of Agra. Even though this happened in the 17th century, similar leaders with Awareness centred around themselves can be seen before and even in the 21st century! We have read and seen the ego-centric behaviour of some dictators and how millions have suffered torture and death at their hands. Greed for wealth and power blinds them completely. From our earlier analogy of muddy water, these people sit at the bottom of the glass and are represented by a thick black line.

CORPORATE CHEATERS

Turning our attention to the corporate world, the greed and self-centred nature of some senior leaders is well known. For example:

In the 1990s, the bursting of the NASDAQ bubble revealed the underlying corporate accounting scandals. As a result, top executives from Enron, Qwest, Tyco, and many other renowned corporations were found guilty and sent to prison. Dennis Kozlowski of Tyco International, beat Wall Street's expectations, consistently over many years, though through fraudulent means. He cheated his company and was making millions of dollars on the side. However, the long arm of the law catches the criminals eventually. Dennis was arrested, convicted, and sent to jail from 2005 to 2014.[6a]

Considered as 'The Big Bull' of the 1990s in India, Harshad Mehta, a stockbroker, became so popular that he featured on the cover page of business magazines that is until his Ponzi schemes were discovered and he was convicted. These corporate examples show men who are selfish. They sit in the middle of the glass of muddy water – the black line with lesser thickness.

Another version of the case is presented here to illustrate that education and experience do not ensure greater self-awareness. One of my friends from school days, Kishore Rathore (*name changed*), moved to the USA in 1974, after his graduation from one of the Regional Engineering Colleges in India. He returned to India after a ten-year stint on the East Coast. In 2001, I met him at one of the Confederation of Indian Industry (CII) conferences in Bengaluru, India. It was a meeting after almost 30 years. He was then the CEO of a company with annual sales of approximately US $32 million. Later, he invited me for a chat over dinner. We met in one of the finest restaurants in Bengaluru. That gave him a chance to show off his wealth and position. What he told me was surprising. He said that he was not happy with his company and wanted to quit just after six months of taking the CEO's role. I was shocked. I probed and asked him, *"Why do you want to leave? After all, you are the boss!"* He answered, *"I agree that I am the boss, but I don't like my compensation being linked to factors other than the financial results of the company."* I drew a blank and requested him to explain. He said, *"Our board, actually it is the chairman of the board, who decides my compensation based on a dashboard. The dashboard is decided on certain criteria I need to fulfil. The criteria include factors like sales growth, increase in profitability, the introduction of new products, societal responsibility, employee and customer satisfaction. Targets are set based on the real potential that* exists and the strategic focus area of the company. The weightage assigned for each measure is not uniform but is related to the Vision, Mission, and Values of the company."

I probably asked the wrong question, as the discussion turned very technical. I thought for a moment and said, *"That sounds like a very logical and powerful dashboard for a CEO. Your board seems very forward-looking. The dashboard seems to be a copybook style balanced scorecard. How does it hurt you?"* Kishore said, *"Jaggu, you don't understand. I am here to make money for my family, and myself, not to satisfy some needs of society, employees, and customers. I would like to get out in three years with a couple of million dollars in my kitty. I don't believe in long-term relationships and the company's Values and Purpose. Do you know the old man, our founder and chairman? He has given a weightage of 50% to measures related to society, employees, and customers altogether? He doesn't understand that we are in business to make money and not for social welfare. When he explained these details to me at the time of my interview, I thought he was trying to impress me with his concern for the community, employees, and customers. I was wrong."* He paused for a few seconds and then said, *"He has become too old."* He seemed agitated and disgusted when he said 'old'.

Despite his excellent academic background, and his years of business experience, his awareness of himself was at the level '1' and had operated from that stance all along. In my opinion, the only mistake the founder and chairman made was in choosing Kishore as the CEO of the company.

I thanked Kishore for the dinner and moved on. I felt sorry for him and prayed and hoped for the best things in life for him. He is probably at the surface level of the muddy glass of water.

The question may arise whether such a leader, operating from *Level 1* would ever have any followers? Generally, they are not good at maintaining healthy relationships. However, even the worst leader may have many followers. The number of followers is no indication of the leader's qualities. The followers may be under some compulsion, or they may be entertaining similar priorities of purely self-centred benefits. Such leaders will not reach the Leaders' Hall of Fame. You will notice that the HEART of leadership is very likely to be missing or yet to germinate in them.

Level 2 – Community and sometimes country: The second level of Self-Awareness is at the Community and Country level. The awareness is beyond the body, mind, intellect, and family. Such leaders identify themselves as members of the society, and the environment around them. The 'My' part extends beyond the family to the community they belong and, in some cases, to the country they are born. At this level, the leaders strive not only to better themselves and their families but also work to improve the status of people in the society and the community around them. Higher the awareness, superior is the field in which the leader operates, wishing well for the whole community. They would support a just cause that benefits the community in a peaceful way. They appreciate others' perspectives and concerns and try to work out win-win solutions.

When the awareness includes the country, the leaders can identify fully with national priorities and citizens' wellbeing. They are conscious of the fact that unless the nation and its citizens prosper, they cannot lead a happy life themselves. Their awareness is well-grounded in the principle 'You win, I win'. They feel a moral responsibility towards the country and work for the wellbeing of all citizens. They do not wait to be prompted but are proactive in their actions to help the country progress. They think in terms of the company's contribution towards the public exchequer and the GDP. They place the country's priorities before their own. The leaders at this level seem to agree with President John F. Kennedy who said, *"Ask not what your country can do for you – ask what you can do for your country"* The qualities of Humility, Excellence, Action, Respect, and commitment to Teamwork radiate from them. The Hall of Fame is assured for the HEART Leaders.

The spread of leaders who are at this level of awareness could be compared to a buffet in which the menu has been carefully planned to please the taste buds of different guests. At a minimum level, it might include five entrées with a dessert, and at the lavish end, it may include 15 entrées, with an array of desserts.

Level 3 - All beings in the Universe: Before I proceed with the discussion on Awareness at Level 3, I want to briefly touch upon my understanding of Spirituality and Religion, and what I mean by Universal Awareness.

For centuries, human beings have been in the pursuit of everlasting happiness and peace. They are constantly trying to get away from sorrow and unrest. Is there any magic potion that will guarantee the fulfilment of this desire? From time-to-time various prophets and seers from different parts of the world, independent of each other, deeply pondered questions like, *'What is happiness?'*, *'Why does happiness not last forever?'*, and *'How does one remain in a steady state of peace?'* During deep contemplation, they discovered that peace and happiness are not the functions of worldly objects, but a state of the mind. The world of objects, however attractive it may be, can only provide temporary satisfaction and happiness. This is because the objects that seem to provide happiness are not permanent, and hence the joy one experiences while using them is also not permanent. Consequently, one jumps from object to object, relationship to relationship, aspiration to aspiration in the hope of finding permanent happiness and peace. However, a lifetime invested in such pursuits does not give the desired results. This leads one to further questions, such as:

'Who am I?'

'What is the purpose of life?'

'How and where can I find True happiness and peace?'

The seers of yore did not have a well-equipped laboratory to carry out their research and conduct experiments. Instead, they used the power of concentration, contemplation, and meditation. Once they got the answers, they taught what they experienced to all humanity. These Masters realised that they were the subject and not the object of their research. They discovered themselves as Consciousness or Awareness - formless, subtler than space, omnipotent, omniscient, omnipresent, infinite, and eternal bliss. Some called it God, Soul,

Almighty, or Supreme Self. The body, mind, and intellect are instruments they are born with, sustained through the lifetime, and discarded at the culmination of one's earthly journey. They further realised that true and everlasting happiness and peace is elusive because of our ignorance; ignorance of not knowing who we really are. Success lies in realising that we are the Supreme Self. The path to this realisation is through the purification of our minds. Religion helps in bringing about discipline at the body-mind levels and to help us progress in our spiritual pursuits. Just as all rivers ultimately reach the sea, so also the different paths enunciated by different Masters of various religions lead us to the same supreme divine principle. The religions could be different, but the underlying spiritual Truth is the same. The religious highways to God are built on the common spiritual foundation of *'Love All and Serve All.'* The primary step in this level of awareness is *'Selflessness'.* [6b]

Ray Chambers, one of the billionaires and top dealmakers on Wall Street, echoes similar thoughts with his 'Five Keys to Happiness'. These are:

1. *Be in the moment.*

2. *Better to be loving than to be right.*

3. *Be a spectator to your own thoughts, particularly when emotional.*

4. *Be grateful.*

5. *Be serviceable to others.* [6c]

The leaders whose awareness reaches its full expanse, embrace the entire universe as their very own. There is no distinction of mine and yours. Such leaders show complete empathy towards fellow beings, respect for both animate and inanimate, and identify themselves as the underlying pure Awareness and not just the body, mind, and intellect. Such leaders experience the hand of unknown energy, call it a Spirit, or a God that is Omnipresent, Omnipotent, and Omniscient. They see the undivided Infinite Divinity, everywhere and in everyone. They realise *'That'* — this is the only Reality, the eternal Awareness that uses the instruments of body, mind, and intellect to accomplish all tasks. Such leaders realise that they are not separate from other beings. So, they are desirous of happiness, peace, and prosperity for all. They have no selfish interests. Their actions are governed by Selflessness. They are constantly committed to *'selfless service'* and embody the maxim, *'Service to Man is Service to God'*. Such leaders reach the highest status of Inspiring Leader. Such leaders are not enamoured by any praise, fame, or recognition. They are neither overjoyed at winning a Nobel Prize, or being called a saint, nor do they feel sad if people do not consider them as an Inspiring Leader. They always maintain equanimity and abide by Universal Awareness.

The band spread at this level of awareness ranges from a simple banana tree at one end of the spectrum and a banyan tree at the other end. Banana trees are so humble that they sacrifice themselves completely for the wellbeing of humanity. The flower, raw banana, ripe fruit, stem, leaves, and even the dried layers of the trunk are useful. The tree is totally selfless. At the other end is the banyan tree, which provides shade and comfort to all human beings and animals. It lets its roots (*followers*) grow fully into big trees under its patronage.

Prophets from different parts of the world and many others identified themselves with the supreme awareness and worked with that worldview. Consequently, followers flocked to them from all over the world, irrespective of age, caste, colour, culture, ethnicity, gender, income, language, nationality, race, and religion. People experience a magnetic pull by such a leader's love, generosity, and compassion. They follow the Inspiring Leader even after their beloved leader physically leaves this ephemeral world. I term these as *inspiring leaders*, who realise this spiritual truth and shape their goals and actions — some label them as role models. For them, the HEART attributes are already a part of their DNA.

In an article titled 'Enlightened Leadership - A Matter of Heart, Mind and Soul', Professor Peter Pruzan from the Copenhagen Business School and his journalist wife Kirsten Pruzan Mikkelsen write:

> *"An international leadership-authority we interviewed didn't hesitate for a moment when asked about the purpose of business organizations, 'It is to serve human needs. Period!' He added, 'Spiritual-based leaders respect others. They are guided by the fundamental ethic: Service to others comes before serving oneself. Individuals and organisations grow when they give themselves to others, and relationships improve when there is a focus on serving the other.'"* [6d]

Their research across five continents and a variety of religious backgrounds shows that leaders who have a spiritual view of life and lead their business from that perspective are truly great as they can integrate the purpose of life with the external world of objects, emotions, and thoughts, and the internal world of consciousness. Spirituality and rationality go hand in hand — for such Leaders 'All work is God's work' as emphasised by Sri Sathya Sai Baba.

"To lead from a spiritual basis means to lead with your heart, your mind and your soul. Our research shows that leaders of all kinds – not only in business, but also in government, public and private administration, hospitals, NGOs, etc. can achieve success, recognition, peace of mind and happiness, while at the same time serve the needs of all those affected by their leadership, when they lead with wisdom, from a spiritual basis." [6d]

TEAMING WITH GOD

Dr. APJ Abdul Kalam, the eleventh President of India (2002-2007) is another great leader who fully accomplished his vision for his profession and his nation. He raised his capability by fifty per cent, by partnering with God! He writes in his autobiography *'Wings of Fire'*:

"I have always been a religious person in the sense that I maintain a working partnership with God. I was aware that the best work required more ability than I possessed, and therefore I needed help that only God could give me. I made a true estimate of my ability, then raised it by 50% and put

myself in God's hands. In this partnership, I have always received all the power I needed, and in fact, have felt it flowing through me. Today, I can affirm that the kingdom of God is within you in the form of this power, to help achieve your goals and realise your dreams." [6e]

"A Spiritual person is one when he closes his eyes finds peace within, and when he opens his eyes his attitude is: what can I do for you?" — Swami Ranganathananda, President (1998-2005), Ramakrishna Math and Mission, India.

During my college days, I heard an interesting story related to Socrates. He was keen to examine his life and discover his true Self, *"Who am I?"*

One day, Socrates was seriously contemplating his quest to discover who he really was. He was so engrossed in his thoughts that while walking on the streets of Athens, he collided with a security guard. The guard was very upset. He caught Socrates by his neck and asked in an angry tone, *"Don't you have eyes? Who are you?"* Socrates replied, *"That's exactly what I want to find out. If you find out, then please let me also know!"*

"As our awareness grows, so we grow." — Anonymous

There are many leaders whose leadership could be considered as truly inspiring, such as those whom we have discussed in the previous five chapters: Abraham Lincoln, Jamsetji Tata, Mahatma Gandhi, Nelson Mandela, Mother Teresa, JRD Tata, Martin Luther King Jr., President Dr. Abdul Kalam, Swami Vivekananda, and Sri

Sathya Sai Baba. However, I have captured brief accounts of only three of the most Inspiring Leaders of the last century to give a fair idea of what legacy they have left behind. There is a lot more about them, several volumes have been written, but here I am conveying only the points that have had a great influence on me.

SERVICE TO JESUS

I saw Mother Teresa for the first time in Jamshedpur, India sometime in 1980-81, when she had come to the 75th Anniversary celebrations of the Rotary International, as the Chief Guest. She was stunningly simple, her face beaming with peace and equipoise. It was radiating a divine glow with an aura that spread like the fragrance of a bunch of jasmine or tuberose flowers.

In the year 1931, at the age of 21, young Anjezë Gonxhe Bojaxhiu came to India from Albania. She came as a novice to Darjeeling and after her Profession of Vows was deputed to the Loreto Convent. She was a teacher and taught Catechism and Geography for many years prior to her appointment as Vice-Principal there. As a teacher, she was known to be a cheerful, happy workmate, with a high sense of humour. She was zestful and hard-working. Above all, she was a woman of deep faith and prayer.

In September 1946, she was travelling to Darjeeling by train to attend her annual retreat. She heard Jesus's call asking her to step into the slums of Kolkata to serve Him in helping the poorest of the poor. She took permission from Mother Gertrude Kennedy, the

Superior General in Rathfarnham, Ireland, and the Archbishop of Kolkata and started on her new mission.

Imagine the number of trials and tribulations a young nun must have faced in a foreign country. Mother Teresa's unquestionable faith in Jesus gave her the necessary energy and enthusiasm to carry out her mission. Although she had initially faced opposition from some locals, people soon recognised her selfless service to the poor and those left on the streets of Kolkata, with no one to care for them. Although she had no funds, she received the support of God as she had partnered with Jesus! By divine intervention, many volunteers came forward and provided regular physical and financial support.

On the 7th October 1950, Mother Teresa received permission from the Holy See to start her own order, The Missionaries of Charity, whose primary task was to love and care for those persons nobody was prepared to look after. In 1965, the charity became an International Religious Family by a decree of Pope Paul VI.

The Society of Missionaries has spread all over the world, including the former Soviet Union and Eastern European countries. They provide effective help to the poorest of the poor and undertake relief work in the wake of natural catastrophes such as floods, epidemics, and famine, and for refugees in several countries across Asia, Africa, and Latin America. The order also has houses in North America, Europe, and Australia, where they take care of shut-ins, alcoholics, homeless, and AIDS sufferers.

The Missionaries of Charity throughout the world are aided and assisted by co-workers who became an official International Association on the 29th March 1969. By the 1990s, there were over one million co-workers in more than 40 countries. Along with the co-workers, the Missionaries of Charity try to follow Mother Teresa's spirit and charisma in their families.

Mother Teresa's work has been globally recognised and acclaimed. She has received several awards and distinctions, including the Pope John XXIII Peace Prize (1971), the Nehru Prize for promotion of international peace and understanding (1972), the Balzan Prize (1979), and the Templeton and Magsaysay Awards. [6f]

Subsequently, The Nobel Committee and the Government of India honoured her with the Nobel Prize for Peace in 1979, and the Bharat Ratna, the highest civilian award in 1980, respectively.

She is a clear example of an Inspiring Leader.

THE REAL POWER OF SELF

Mohandas Karamchand Gandhi, better known as Mahatma (Great Soul) Gandhi, is another example of an Inspiring Leader most respected and regarded by Indians as the Father of the Nation. Born on the 2nd October 1869 in Porbandar under British-ruled India, Gandhi lived on three continents (Asia, Europe, and Africa) over the subsequent eight decades, and inspired people from all continents with his unique worldview.

Gandhi said, *"A man is but the product of his thoughts. What he thinks, he becomes."* He strongly believed in the strength of thought more than physical capacity. Even though he looked very frail physically, he had the power of an elephant and a lion combined. He could go on a fast for days, walk several miles, and remain silent, all for a noble cause or a profound principle. He was multi-dimensional, amiable, assertive, fearless, mindful, principled, righteous, and spiritual.

At school, I was greatly influenced by Gandhi, and fifty years later, his influence still pervades. Based on the famous sayings of Mahatma Gandhi, which are often quoted by other leaders, we can understand what he stood for, and what his values were.

"Serve humanity but with humility."

"Change yourself if you want to bring about a change in the world."

"There is a sufficiency in the world for man's need but not for man's greed."

"The best way to find yourself is to lose yourself in the service of others."

"Honest disagreement is often a good sign of progress."

"Non-violence is a weapon of the strong." [6g]

Mahatma Gandhi lived the values that were very close to his Heart. Some of them are anecdotally discussed here. [6h]

ADHERENCE TO TRUTH

As a child of seven, Gandhi was greatly influenced by a play on King Harishchandra. This ancient Indian king considered Truth as a virtue and was willing to do anything to adhere to it. Once the great Sage Vishwamitra wanted to test King Harishchandra to see whether the king would give up his adherence to values and utter a lie while facing terrible calamities. However, the king stuck to his values and was willing to suffer. He sold his wife and son as slaves but did not give up Truth. The child Gandhi wanted to see the play again and again, but how often could he get permission from his father? Instead, he acted the role of the king and never got tired of it! Mahatma Gandhi's autobiography, *'The Story of My Experiments with Truth'*, is proof of this value even today. His book is a spiritual journey he took to realise the fundamental principle of Truth. He often said, *"Truth is God"*.

RESPECT FOR TIME

Gandhi was a stickler for time and never wasted a single minute. While in prison, in Yerawada Jail (Pune), he fully utilised his time by writing his views, and articles related to various topics. As part of his daily routine at his Ashrams at Sabarmati (Ahmedabad, Gujarat) or Sevagram (Wardha, Maharashtra), he planned his schedule in a way that he could spare time to practise meditation, say his prayers, take long walks, attend to domestic animals in the Ashram, practise Naturopathy, meet Leaders of political parties, read the Bhagavad Geeta, and live his values every day, without exception.

Following Non-Violence

Ahimsa (non-violence) to Gandhi did not just mean causing no physical harm to other beings. It meant much more. Ahimsa meant causing no harm to others even in thought and word, not just the deed. When he applied this principle to his life, it became the path to pursue the Truth or God. In politics, he used it to gain political freedom for India from British Rule.

He never believed in the philosophy of an 'eye for an eye' for it only blinds the world. The world for the first time woke up to the clarion call for freedom from foreign rule, and to achieve this through a peaceful and non-violent movement, which was called 'Satyagraha', meaning a fight for Truth. As a lawyer he had started the non-violent movement in South Africa between 1893 and 1914 - the years he was practising in that country as a lawyer. After returning to India in 1915, he transformed Satyagraha into one of the greatest movements for India's sovereignty. Gandhi was arrested several times and sentenced to jail by the Imperial British Rule.

When Gandhi chose a location for his Ashram, near Ahmedabad, he decided on a piece of land near the banks of the River Sabarmati, as it had the Sabarmati Central Jail next to it. He thought it would be helpful as the Satyagrahis (those who followed Satyagraha) were frequently sent there by the British Raj, so it was useful to be living close by!

Martin Luther King Jr., one of the iconic leaders from the USA, revered Gandhi, and his ideals. He accepted the practice of a non-violent movement as a means of bringing social change in the modern world's oldest democracy.

"If humanity is to progress, Gandhi is inescapable. He lived, thought, and acted, inspired by the vision of humanity evolving toward a world of peace and harmony. We may ignore him at our own risk." — Martin Luther King Jr. [6i]

ALL ARE EQUAL

Gandhi strongly believed that all human beings are equal and are driven by the same divine spark of God. He looked at everyone as God in human form. He shunned the idea of untouchables and called them 'Harijan' meaning 'God's People' (Hari is a name given to God by Hindus). To prove his point, he went and lived in their homes. He washed, cleaned, and nursed a person who suffered from leprosy while in South Africa. To him, all names and forms were manifestations of God.

Gandhi's faith in following Truth and Non-violence was unshakable. He lived his life true to this faith. No wonder he was called 'Mahatma Gandhi'.

LOVE IS GOD, GOD IS LOVE

As recent as the turn of the century, the world witnessed a spiritual phenomenon by the name of Sri Sathya Sai Baba.

He was born as Sathya Narayana Raju on the 23rd November 1926, in the remote village of Puttaparthi, in the erstwhile Madras Presidency of British-ruled India. Even as a child, young Sathya was vastly different. Not only was he extraordinarily intelligent, but also always full of love and compassion. In primary school, he helped his classmates in diverse ways. He not only excelled in academics but also in dramatics, music, and poetry. Though from a poor family, he would give his books to his needy classmates, give away his food to the hungry and physically challenged, help the elderly in their daily chores, and even gather the young children to reform the village. Through all these simple yet profound acts, he distinctly displayed his empathy and foresight.

All was reasonably well until the morning of the 20th October 1940, when something remarkable happened. Sathya, only 13 years old then, left home for school as usual, but within minutes returned. Standing on the doorstep, he flung aside the bag containing his schoolbooks and in ringing tones declared to his astonished family members, "*I am no longer your Sathya. I don't belong to you. I have my mission. I am going. I can no longer stay here.*" From that day began his mission of universal transformation through love and service. Over the next 60 years, he remained supremely committed to this task, not only by personally interacting with over two million people and lecturing to several million across the length and breadth of India, but also through the establishment of institutions and initiating projects that served as role models for addressing the basic issues of education, healthcare, and drinking water supply in the world's largest democracy. However, he never took credit for the stupendous tasks undertaken. Instead, he gave the credit to his mother – Easwaramma, and how his work was to fulfill three promises that he made to her – providing a hospital in the village (Puttaparthi), a school to be built for the village children, and the village to be provided with a drinking water facility.

What appears as a casual fulfilment of mundane wishes, was a behemoth task of single-handedly impacting the lives of over 25 million people in a span of 50 years. Let us briefly look at how this was accomplished and the vision behind this phenomenal story that unfolded in the second half of the last century. [6j]

TEMPLES OF HEALING

On the 23rd November 1990, on his 65th birthday, Sri Sathya Sai Baba announced that in a year, a super speciality hospital providing tertiary-level healthcare at no cost to the beneficiaries would be set up by the Sri Sathya Sai Central Trust just outside Puttaparthi in the Anantapur District, Andhra Pradesh, India.[6k] At the time of the announcement, the plans weren't ready, the proposed site was not levelled, and no related infrastructure was in place. Everyone wondered if the promise could be met. However, exactly a year later, the then Prime Minister of India, P. V. Narasimha Rao inaugurated the majestic 180-bed hospital building on the sprawling grounds and equipped with the latest medical infrastructure. Since then, the hospital, Sri Sathya Sai Institute of Higher Medical Sciences, has grown in scale and the mission has added another super speciality hospital at Whitefield in Bengaluru, India's IT Capital, in January 2001, which was inaugurated by the then Prime Minister of India, Atal Bihari Vajpayee. Over the last three decades, the two hospitals have performed over 500,000 surgeries and treated over 2.5 million outpatients from across India and South Asia in cardiac, neurology, nephrology, urology, ophthalmology, gastroenterology, orthopedic and other super-specialisations at absolutely no cost to the beneficiaries. In terms of the market value calculated in dollar terms, the quantum of free healthcare provided by these institutions would amount to a philanthropic contribution of over US$ 10 billion.

This journey of alleviating the sicknesses and diseases of the poor through scientific approaches had begun 35 years earlier. The first Sri Sathya Sai General Hospital inaugurated on the 4th October 1956 at Puttaparthi was the only healthcare facility in the entire region within a radius of 30 kilometres. This eight-bed hospital providing primary care has since grown into a 100-bed hospital, providing free primary and secondary care services across seven departments. In the last 65 years, this hospital alone has benefitted over 10 million outpatients from free healthcare services.

Sri Sathya Sai Baba's commitment to the poorest section of the society and remains a testament to this cause. He attracted luminaries from the most respected corners of the world, be it John Hopkins Healthcare Centre USA, All-India Institute of Medical Sciences, and Duke University, USA to be part of an international medical committee to bring his vision to fruition. Based on the deliberations of the committee, it was decided that the setting up of a multi-discipline super-speciality hospital would serve the objective of providing the best quality medical care to the poorest sections of society. It was this vision that took the shape of the two super speciality hospitals I previously mentioned.

However, more than this, it is Baba's approach to medical care that has been truly inspiring. His guidelines for a humanised holistic healthcare system include the five principles of Universal Healthcare,

Free Healthcare, Preventive Healthcare, Comprehensive Healthcare, and Loving Healthcare. He repeatedly emphasised that state-of-the-art healthcare should be available to all people, irrespective of caste, religion, nationality, or economic status. In the absence of government-sponsored health insurance or comprehensive social security schemes, the lower-income sections of the population are the most affected by high costs of healthcare. Consequently, they are pushed to the brink of poverty or get trapped in indebtedness. During the inauguration of the Super Speciality Hospital at Puttaparthi on the 22nd November 1991, Baba said:

"This hospital has been set up to provide relief to villagers. No distinction is made, however, between villages and cities. Diseases do not afflict only villagers. They make no territorial distinctions. Likewise, there will be no differentiation in providing relief. Our intention is to provide relief to all."

The Sathya Sai Philosophy lays special emphasis on preventive care and advocates educating the people on healthy living habits and spreading awareness among them. Ministering to physical, mental, and psychological health may not suffice. The aim should also be to energise the spirit of the patient – the Divine force in him/her that sustains the physical, mental, and psychological systems. Developing faith in God, cultivation of human values, and fostering love in the heart are ingredients of spiritual health delivery. It further stresses that medical care should be administered with patience, compassion, and a sense of service. Baba has repeatedly exhorted that if the doctor is full of love and compassion, God works through him/her and, therefore, doctors should endeavour to become receptacles of Divine Power during their healing process.

Dr. Michael Nobel, Chairperson, Nobel Prize Committee, who visited the super speciality hospital at Puttaparthi in 2001, observed:

"A one-of-a-kind combination of hi-tech, state of the art medical facility offering the top-of-the-line treatment for free to the masses of the people who would never normally have such a chance in life. An awe-inspiring achievement! Thank you, Baba on behalf of mankind."

Underscoring the replicability of Baba's Medical Mission, the lessons that institutions of higher medicine in the east and west can learn from his hospitals, Dr. Mitchell Krucoff from Duke University, observed:

"Like shining stars in the durkest of nights, Baba's Hospitals in Puttaparthi and Bangalore (Bengaluru) not only live the answer to that question in the free care they deliver every day, but also as examples of how much God is ready to teach us about the alleviation of human suffering through optimal medical care. He (Baba) has built these programmes, all we have to do is to open our eyes and see ... to the western world of modern medicine, what a blessing it is to have such a guiding light."

TEMPLES OF LEARNING

Way back in the early 1960s, Sri Sathya Sai Baba had foreseen the need for a values-based education programme and had taken concrete steps to implement the same into a formal education system known as the Sri Sathya Sai System of Values-Based Integral Education. Speaking at the Maharani's Women's College in Mysore in September 1963, he said:

> *"Education is not for mere living; it is for life, a fuller life, a more meaningful, and a more worthwhile life. There is no harm if it is also for a gainful employment; but the educated man must be aware that existence is not all, that gainful employment is not all."* [6m]

In June 1966, Baba was at Anantapur, a town 60 miles from Puttaparthi, at the invitation of a high school for girls. The plight of the girls who had to go to distant places for higher education, and the secular education (bereft of values) for which they were spending much time and money, touched him. He announced that there would soon be a women's college in Anantapur. On the 22nd July 1968, he laid the foundation of the college for women at Anantapur. At a time when gender equality issues had not even surfaced in the field of education in India, he envisioned the importance of educating women who would serve as the foundation for the building of the nation. Baba's main aim in starting a women's college was to emphasise that if a woman is educated, the entire family benefits from her knowledge and wisdom, as she plays an important role in moulding the future generations of the family into responsible citizens. While inaugurating the college building for women in the presence of then President of India, V.V. Giri and his wife Saraswathi Giri, Baba declared that the college would soon be transformed into a university. On the 9th June 1969, the Sri Sathya Sai Arts and Science College for men was inaugurated in the city of Bengaluru. A decade later, he laid the foundation stone for the College of Arts, Science and Commerce at Puttaparthi. The three campuses eventually merged under the umbrella of the Sri Sathya Sai Institute of Higher Learning (SSSIHL) on the 22nd November 1981, as a deemed university, with Sri Sathya Sai Baba as its Founder Chancellor.

The philosophical cornerstone of the education system propounded by Baba is the concept of 'Educare'. He drew a distinction between what has traditionally been conceived to be 'education' and what he referred to as Educare. He said that educationists who merely read books and passed on the contents to students were not fulfilling the real goals of education. Real education is that which promotes unity, equality, and peaceful co-existence with fellow human beings. It flows from the heart and is termed as Educare. According to the Oxford English Dictionary, 'education' is derived from its Latin root 'educare' which means 'to rear or to bring up'. Educare itself can be traced to the Latin root words, 'e' and 'ducere'. Together, 'e-ducere' means to 'pull out' or 'to lead forth'. Hence, the word educare is used to communicate the teaching method through which children and adults are encouraged to 'think' and 'draw out' information from within. The inspiration for using the term educare by Sri Sathya Sai Educational Institutions for its programmes has come from a discourse of Sathya Sai Baba in which he explained the meaning of true education. On the valedictory function of the First International Conference of Sathya Sai Schools on the 21st November 2001, he said:

> *"The word 'education' is derived from the Latin root 'educare'. While education refers to a collection of worldly facts, educare is to bring out from within. Education is for a living while educare is for life. Educare has two aspects, the worldly and the spiritual. Worldly education brings out the latent knowledge pertaining to the physical world. Spiritual education brings out the inherent divinity in humans. So, both worldly and spiritual education is essential, without which the human life has no value."*

The best way to teach values is by practice. Therefore, teachers must inspire students to practise values in their daily life by living as role models for them to emulate. Hence, the professional life and personal life of the teacher must be well integrated and exemplary. Values-oriented education fructifies only when teachers have faith in it. As the teacher, so the taught. It is to be recognised that in all educational activities and particularly in values promotion and dissemination, what counts most is the teacher. Committed teachers can be the best guides, friends, and philosophers to students.

The Sri Sathya Sai Educational Institutions believe in integrating ethics and values as the undercurrent of every subject. Baba's Educational Institutions adopted the integrated approach of values-oriented education that aimed at inculcation of values through all academic programmes and activities The teacher integrated the relevant values in the daily lessons and in other activities outside the classroom – both curricular and co-curricular.

The proof of the pudding is in the eating, and the impact of such a system can be measured by the transformational change it brings in its students, beyond their years at the alma mater. In 2010, a study conducted by SSSIHL, in collaboration with external experts, revealed many interesting aspects with respect to the alumni.[6n] Nine of every ten alumni who participated in the study felt that their experience at SSSIHL contributed significantly towards one or more of the following: patience and perseverance, leadership, organising time effectively, and inspiring others by example. Seven in every ten alumni who participated in the study felt that their experience at SSSIHL contributed very significantly towards one or more of the following: integrity, work ethics, concern for society and environment, dealing with different types of people, and working in teams. Most of the alumni continued to undertake one or more of the following activities that they were exposed to while at SSSIHL regularly in their daily life: prayer and meditation, yoga, sports and exercises, scriptural study and devotional singing, poor feeding, and community involvement.

It can thus be said that the influence of the ambience, the approach to education and the philosophy of life in general imbibed by the students while at Sri Sathya Sai Educational Institutions influenced their thinking and attitudes to work in their respective professions. Emphasising this significant contribution in redefining education at the university level in India, the then President of India, Dr. APJ

Abdul Kalam, observed at the XXI Convocation of SSSIHL, on the 22nd November 2002:

"The purpose of real education is to initiate a learning process that transforms students into good human beings with knowledge and value systems. Is values-based education possible? Sri Sathya Sai Institute of Higher Learning has given an answer in the affirmative. I would like to congratulate the Institute for this noble education."

The experience and results of the last four decades seem to indicate that this novel and memorable experiment in education has been significantly successful in achieving the goals and objectives with which it was started. However, the true impact in terms of the intensity and scale can perhaps be felt when this model of education is emulated and practised on a much wider and larger scale across educational institutions in the country and elsewhere. The Peer Team of the National Accreditation and Assessment Council (NAAC) from the University Grants Commission, the apex regulator of higher education institutions in India, made a similar observation in its report submitted in March 2003:

"The Peer Team feels that this Institute (SSSIHL) stands out as a crest jewel among the University Education System in the country and this model is worthy of emulation by institutions of higher learning in India and elsewhere, so that these benefits would be reaped fast and on the widest possible scale."

Complementing the education ecosystem under Baba's direct guidance is a network of 140 Sathya Sai Schools in India and 25 other countries including Thailand, Zambia, Paraguay, Chile, Mexico, Ecuador, New Zealand, Venezuela, Brazil, UK, Canada, Philippines, Taiwan, Argentina, Australia, Indonesia, South Africa, and Nepal. These institutions are all based on the philosophy of Education in Human Values as propounded by Sri Sathya Sai Baba and have educated over 55,000 students every year for the last 30 plus years.

ELIXIR OF LIFE

On the morning of the 22nd November 1994, a felicitation function had been arranged to acknowledge the contributions of a senior physician of the Sri Sathya Sai Institute of Higher Medical Sciences at Puttaparthi. P.V. Narasimha Rao, then Prime Minister of India, was also present. In his address, Sri Sathya Sai Baba made a direct reference to the perennial drinking water problem in Rayalaseema, an arid, drought-ridden belt in the Anantapur district of Andhra Pradesh, India. But there was no response or reaction from the government. A few months later, during another function, Sathya Sai Baba announced that he would take up the project himself. Eighteen months later this became a reality. Safe drinking water flowed out of thousands of water taps in 730 villages of the parched district of Anantapur. The Sri Sathya Sai Drinking Water Supply Project provided water to over a million people who had lived all their lives at the edge of drought and despair. But it was not the government, whose bounden task it was that provided this, but the action taken by the leader of a non-profit trust. 6p

Let us see how this mammoth task, unprecedented in the history of Independent India, unfolded.

The Anantapur District in southwest Andhra Pradesh has a population of nearly four million and is the second most arid district in India after the Thar Desert in Rajasthan (Northwest India). Successive droughts and heavy withdrawal of groundwater for irrigation had resulted in the continuous lowering of groundwater from 50 meters in the 1960s to 150 meters by 2010. Chronic water scarcity adversely affected food security and income-earning opportunities, particularly of the rural poor. For half a century since Independence, the government did not take any substantial steps. That's when a unique collaboration emerged in 1994. Sri Sathya Sai Baba, born in that region nearly 70 years earlier, decided to commission a project to provide drinking water to the entire Anantapur District, the seventh-largest (by area) district in India among 718 districts. The implementation was given to Larsen & Toubro, India's premier construction company. Sri Sathya Sai Central Trust provided the entire fund of INR 3 billion to complete the project (approximately US$ 60 million)

The colossal scale of the project involved a pipeline of 1,400 miles, construction of 268 overhead reservoirs (capacities up to 300,000 litres), 145 ground-level reservoirs (up to 10,00,000 litres capacity), 40 booster pumping stations, 280 deep bore-wells, and 13 infiltration wells to meet the current and future demand factoring in the population growth for the next 30 years. It provided 1,700 stand posts and 1,000 concrete cisterns to enable 1.25 million people to collect safe drinking water every single day. And all this was accomplished in a record time of 16 months. According to an impact evaluation study for the Asian Development Bank (ADB), the cost would have escalated by an additional INR 3 billion, and project completion would have taken 60 months instead of 16 months, but for the synergies that emerged from a common purpose shared by all stakeholders. This ADB Study also indicated that the project demonstrated true partnership, transferability, replicability, and sustainability. [69]

After the successful completion of the Anantapur Drinking Water Supply Project, which was inaugurated by then President of India Dr. Shankar Dayal Sharma, a similar collaborative approach was followed to provide water to 450 upland and tribal habitations in East Godavari and West Godavari Districts of coastal Andhra Pradesh, and to 320 villages in the Districts of Medak and Mahbubnagar (the eighth largest district in India), in the southern state of Telangana. The most notable of the projects in terms of beneficiary scale was the one that provided drinking water to 8 million people suffering from an acute shortage in the metropolis of Chennai, the capital of the state of Tamil Nadu. In fact, Chennai has been nicknamed the 'Detroit of India' due to the presence of major automobile manufacturing units and allied industries around the city.

The stellar implementation and impact of these projects have been acknowledged by the World Water Forum in Japan (2003) and Mexico (2006) as exemplars of public-private partnership, and among the best local action projects to achieve Millennium Development Goals. It was because of Baba's phenomenal vision and passion that in a span of just 12 years, over 12.5 million citizens from three states and multiple districts of India benefitted from drinking water supplies. This is the equivalent of the populations of New Zealand, Switzerland, and Qatar put together!

LOVE ALL, SERVE ALL

In addition to these mammoth projects, Baba founded Sri Sathya Sai Seva Organisations in India in 1965. The word 'Seva' means 'Service' in English. Headquartered at Prasanthi Nilayam, it operates through nearly 6,000 centres in 25 states across India with nearly 600,000 volunteers undertaking service projects in as diverse areas as rural development, women's empowerment, skills training, disaster management, values education, medical relief, and several others. Sri Sathya Sai International Organisation was mandated by Baba to facilitate global public service activities through 2,000 centres across 125 countries. Driven by Baba's directives, this organisational ecosystem operates with the philosophy of 'Love All, Serve All'. Even after the culmination of his earthly sojourn on the 24th April 2011, Baba's Mission continues to revolve around the nucleus of enabling its volunteer members to undertake service activities as a means to their spiritual advancement and to enable them to realise the one underlying Divine principle.

I recognise Sri Sathya Sai Baba as an Inspiring Leader not only because of my personal veneration and interaction with him but also because of the stupendous work he has single-handedly undertaken to implement his vision of a society based on selfless love and service. If viewed dispassionately, it is the selfishness of individuals and institutions, nations, and governments, that is the root cause of the problems the world is currently facing. The remedy lies in placing human beings and their welfare at the core of our life and its purpose, irrespective of our professions and passions, region, or religion. It was this message that Baba brought into the lives of millions of his admirers and followers across the world over six decades. His message and mission as an Inspiring Leader can be summed up through what he said in a discourse delivered to the people of Nairobi, Kenya on the 4th July 1968:

"I have come to light the lamp of love in your hearts, to see that it shines day by day with added lustre. I have not come to speak on behalf of any particular religion like the Hindu Dharma. I have not come on any mission of publicity for any sect or creed or cause; nor have I come to collect followers for any doctrine. I have no plan to attract disciples or devotees into my fold or any fold. I have come to tell you of this Universal unitary faith, this atmic principle (atmic derived from a Sanskrit word 'atma', pronounced aathma — is the spark of divinity), means this Path of Love, this Religion of Love, this Duty of Love, this Obligation to Love."

Who is an Inspiring Leader?

MY FOUR PART REFLECTION

Firstly, the Inspiring Leader is fully aware of one's true Self. He identifies with Pure Awareness and realises that he is not the body, mind, and intellect. He empathises fully with other beings as he sees himself in them. Through reflections, experience, and efforts at personal transformation, his worldview changes to the realisation that he is not a human being seeking divinity, but he is divinity having a human experience.

Secondly, the Inspiring Leader wants peace, health, and happiness for all. He does not fall prey to greed, jealousy, ego, attachment, anger, and other negative tendencies. He works for universal wellbeing rather than selfish benefits.

Thirdly, the Inspiring Leader lives by example. His life is his message. He lives his values every day. Since the past is history and cannot be changed, the future is uncertain and no one has any control over it, he always lives in the present. He plans and works diligently with clear goals in mind. His efforts are genuine, and he is not worried about the outcome.

Lastly, when the Inspiring Leader winds up and leaves his mortal coil, those who flocked around him, and followed him for what he did, continue to carry on his message, even in his absence. They start to live his message.

"The key to growth is the introduction of higher dimensions of consciousness into our awareness." — Lao Tzu.

THE FUTURE LEADERS

Just as a seed has the potential to become a full-grown tree giving leaves, flowers, and fruits, the children of today have the latent potential to be the young leaders of tomorrow.

As adults, it is our moral responsibility to inspire and nurture them with human values. It is our primary duty to lead by example rather than precept. The youth are already technologically advanced. As a result, they have much more information at their fingertips than people of their age a generation back. The human characteristics of Humility, Excellence, Action, Respect, and Teamwork must be cultivated through loving care and actual demonstration of the expected behaviour at home, in school, and on the playground.

As a young manager, I always wanted to be the CEO of an organisation of repute. Way back in 1975, I had shared this desire with one of my early mentors – Sheikh Ali, Head of Human Resources in Tata Motors, Jamshedpur. His advice to me was:

"Observe the great leaders in action and absorb their characteristics. Practise and live those characteristics in day-to-day work and watch for results."

This advice led me to the discovery of the HEART and Soul of Leadership. The real education for me was the fact that the six characteristics discussed in the book have not changed for thousands of years! Even today, they are valid and will continue to remain valid for eons to come.

FIRMLY, I BELIEVE

I firmly believe that Inspiring Leaders live their message and show it through role model behaviour. While leading a team of young managers, I had arranged an outdoor workshop focusing on teamwork in Pune. As a part of the programme, the consultant faculty had included an event called 'Fire Walk'. Literally, the entire team had to walk over the length of a rectangular bed of burning charcoal, 5 feet by 20 feet. Some members were a little hesitant, but when they saw me do it, they were encouraged and completed the task. Let me confess here. The burning charcoal did burn my feet slightly. However, if I had not walked on the fire, it would have burnt the team spirit which I was trying to build. It was more important to lead the team from the front and set an example rather than preach team spirit.

I firmly believe that it is time for the wisdom and maturity of seniors to be channelled into mentoring, coaching, and guiding young managers with Love and demonstrated by Living Our Values every day. There are approximately 2 billion young adults in the world today. Their potential is very high and if harnessed carefully and productively can transform the whole world.

I firmly believe that it is time that we revisit our education systems and revitalise them. Sai Baba often said, *"The End of Education is Character. If health, and wealth are lost, they can be regained. But if character is lost, then everything is lost."* We need to bring in the basic principle of spirituality and not religion into the school curriculums that underscore the oneness of all humanity. The foundation for Universal Awareness must be started, strengthened, and sustained from an early age.

I firmly believe that if we expect the best out of young adults, they will surely rise to that level. Young adults who aspire to become Inspiring Leaders need challenging assignments and opportunities to bring forth their creativity, knowledge, and high energy. The worst is to set low standards of expectations and then blame every other person for mediocre overall performance. Instead, we need to create a challenging atmosphere and ask them to lead.

I firmly believe that the HEART Leaders of tomorrow are already here, just waiting to flap their wings of self-awareness and self-confidence and soar high in the sky. With appropriate encouragement, they can enter the circle of Inspiring Leaders. The participation of millions of young adults and managers, all over the world, in several service programmes related to community development, climate change, animal protection, and helping the distressed through the current Covid-19 pandemic is clear proof of their commitment to improve the wellbeing of all beings.

I firmly believe that young professionals of today will ensure that this beautiful planet is well preserved and protected.

I firmly believe that through the HEART and the SOUL of Inspiring Leadership they will bring happiness and peace in this world.

I firmly believe that they will succeed in this Mission.

समस्ताः लोकः सुखिनो भवन्तु
"Samastha Lokah Sukhino Bhavantu"
(Let all the beings in all the worlds be happy)

References

1a   NASA Science; Space Place; Explore Earth & Space,
NASA Official Kristen Erickson; Programme Manager : Heether Doyle
https://spaceplace.nasa.gov/sun-compare/en/

1b   Raghu Kale, *"Loyalty & Sacrifice – Ushering New Horizons for Business Leaders in the Digital Age"*, page 67, Striking Ideas

1c   3 Reasons LinkedIn is an Awesome Place to Work
*https://theundercoverrecruiter.com/linkedin-culture/
#:~:text=LinkedIn's%20company%20culture%20is%20something,slide%2 0deck%20(see%20below)*

1d   *"Astonishing Power of Humility"*, An exclusive interview with wildly successful Bourne series producer Jeffrey Weiner, as well as new research, highlights the power of humility"
https://scottmautz.com/jason-bourne-science-teaches-us-astonishing-power-humility/

1e   Steven Gambardella, Tolstoy's Moral Lesson, *"The Philosophy of the Three Hermits"*
https://medium.com/the-sophist/tolstoys-moral-lesson-69754892d899

1f   Gen. James L. Anderson, USA (Ret.) and Dave Anderson, *"Becoming a leader of character"*, Morgan James, ISBN   978-1-63047-937-4

1g   C.S.Lewis, *"Mere Christianity"*, Book 3, Chapter 8, *"The Great Sin"*, Kindle Location 1665

1h   Dave Anderson, *"A short story of Great Humility in 500 words"* Mar 13, 2018,   Category: Leadership My Dad's Way, Anderson Leadership Solutions+A26:A27
http://www.andersonleadershipsolutions.com/short-story-great-humility-500-words/

1i   Bradley P. Owens and David R. Hekman, *"How does Leader Humility Influence Team Performance?"* April 2015, The Academy of Management Journal.
*https://www.researchgate.net/publication/
277357402_How_Does_Leader_Humility_Influence_Team_Performance_Expl oring_the_Mechanisms_of_Contagion_and_Collective_Promotion_Focus*

1j   Kharunya Paramaguru, *"5 Great Stories About Nelson Mandela's Humility, Kindness and Courage Remarkable moments recalled by some of the people who knew him best"*, Dec. 06, 2013
https://world.time.com/2013/12/06/5-great-stories-about-nelson-mandelas-humility-kindness-and-courage/

1k   S A Vaneswaran, ex-colleague of Dr. Kalam, DRDO, India, 1982-89, in conversation with author, and in a WhatsApp message.

1l   President Barack Obama's message on the demise of Dr.Kalam, The White House Office of the Press Secretary on July 28, 2015
https://obamawhitehouse.archives.gov/the-press-office/2015/07/28/statement-president-death-former-indian-president-dr-apj-abdul-kalam

1m   An interview with S.Chandrasekhar, Director, Higginbothams Private Limited, Chennai, India

1n   Kevin Leyes, *"Learning to unlearn: The importance of reinventing yourself"*, YEC Council Post, Forbes, April1, 2020
https://www.forbes.com/sites/theyec/2020/04/01/learning-to-unlearn-the-importance-of-reinventing-yourself/?sh=94e980791b9e

1p   Ashley Merryman, *"Leaders are more powerful when they're humble, new research shows"* Washington Post, dated Dec 8,2016
https://www.washingtonpost.com/news/inspired-life/wp/2016/12/08/leaders-are-more-powerful-when-theyre-humble-new-research-shows/

2a   Personal Experience, Story told to me by my school teacher Mrs. Ranganayaki Krishnan, 6th July,2006

2b   Harish Bhatt, *"JRD-flying after excellence"* article published in Economic Times, July 28,2017
https://www.economictimes.indiatimes.com/blogs/et-commentary/jrd-flying-after-excellence/

2c   Good Thoughts, Good Words, Good Deeds, *"A book of Tata Quotes"*, Tata Central Archives, A Division of Tata Services Limited, Pune, India

2d   Ratan Tata's Address at the JRD Quality Value Night 29 July, 2001 from my personal notes and records.

2e   David Mikkelson,Abraham Lincoln and Failure, Legend: Abraham Lincoln endured a steady stream of failure and defeat before becoming President of the United States, Published 12 July 2000
https://www.snopes.com/fact-check/abraham-lincoln-failure/

2f   Lt.Gen (Ret.) Dr.M L Chibber, PVSM, AVSM, PhD, *" Ssi Baba's Mahavakya on Leadership"*, Sri Sathya Sai Books & Publications Trust, ISBN 81-7208-180-4

3a   From personal notes and recollections as Chief of Total Quality and Rengineering, Tata Steel

4a   R M Lala, "For Love Of India: The Life and Times of Jamshedji Tata, Penguin & Viking, ISBN 0-67-005782-7

4b   Good Thoughts, Good Words, Good Deeds, *"A book of Tata Quotes"*, Tata Central Archives, A Division of Tata Services Limited, Pune, India

4c   R M Lala, *"In Search of Ethical Leadership"*, Vision Books, ISBN 81-7094-732-4

4d   R M Lala, "a touch of GREATNESS -Encounters with the Eminent", Viking, ISBN 0-670-91128-3

4e   Personal discussions with Dr. V.M.Mokashi, Professor and Head of Civil Engineering, Visvesvaraya Regional College of Engineering (now named VNIT), Nagpur, India

5a   Atul Gawande, *"The Checklist Manifesto"*, Penguin Viking, ISBN 978-0-670-08440-1

5b   *https://www.thecricketlounge.com/2008/11/5/*

5c   A Century of Trust - Inspiring Legends and Legacies, Reprinted from Reader's Digest Best of Inspiration, July,2005, Tata publication

5d   *https://www.nbccamps.com/basketball.0*

6a   Aaron Levitt, *"The 15 Most Notorious Wall Street Villains"*, September 18, 2014
https://mutualfunds.com/education/biggest-stock-market-villains/

6b   Sri Sathya Sai Media Centre
https://media.radiosai.org/www/

6c   Tom Rapsas, *"The reluctant Billionaire and his 5 Keys to happiness"* September 13, 2018
https://www.patheos.com/blogs/wakeupcall/2018/09/the-reluctant-billionaire-and-his-5-keys-to-happiness/

6d   Professor Peter Pruzan, and Journalist Mrs. Kirsten Pruzan Mikkelsen, "ENLIGHTENED LEADERSHIP, A Matter of Heart, Mind and Soul, Sri Sathya Sai Media Centre",
https://media.radiosai.org/journals/Vol_05/01AUG07/03-coverstory.htm
media.radiosai.org › journals › Vol_05 › 03-coverstory

6e   Dr. APJ Abdul Kalam with Arun Tiwari, *"Wings of fire"* An Autobiography, Universities Press, ISBN 8173711461

6f   From Nobel Lectures, Peace 1971-1980, Editor-in-Charge Tore Frängsmyr, Editor Irwin Abrams, World Scientific Publishing Co., Singapore, 1997
https://www.nobelprize.org/prizes/peace/1979/teresa/facts/

6g   460 Mahatma Gandhi Quotes to Bring the Best Out of You
https://wisdomquotes.com/gandhi-quotes/

6h   Mahatma Gandhi MK, *"An autobiography or The story of my experiments*
      with truth", A Penguin Book, ISBN 0-14-006626-8

      Excerpts from "Biography of Mahatma Gandhi", Comprehensive
      Gandhi website by Gandhian Institutions : Bombay Sarvodaya
      Mandal & Gandhi Research Foundation

      https://www.mkgandhi.org/africaneedsgandhi/
      biography.htm#:~:text=Mohandas%20Karamchand%20Gandhi%20was%20b
      orn,father%20of%20the%20Indian%20Nation.

6i   Becky Little, *"How Martin Luther King Jr. Took Inspiration From Gandhi on*
      Nonviolence"

      https://www.biography.com/news/martin-luther-king-jr-gandhi-nonviolence-
      inspiration

6j   Shah, Shahank and V.E. Ramamoorthy, *Soulful Corporations: A Values*
      Based Approach to Corporate Social Responsibility, Springer Publications, 2013.

6k   A public charitable trust founded by Baba in 1972. It is headquartered
      in Puttaparthi, Andhra Pradesh, India.

6m   Shah, Shashank and G.S. Srirangajaran, *"Sri Sathya Sai University: A*
      Values-based System of Education".

      Indian Ethos and Values in Management, (Eds) R. Nandagopal and Ajith
      Sankar R.N., PSG Institute of Management, Tata Mc Graw Hill, 2010

6n   These included Prof. Peter Pruzan, Professor Emeritus, Copenhagen
      Business School; Mandip Sandhu, former Management Consultant,
      IBM Canada; Sripriya N., Project Manager, Computer Sciences
      Corporation, India; and C. Kundhavi, Principal Systems Analyst,
      Ministry of Information Technology, Government of India. Over 300
      alumni from men's campuses and 450 alumni from the women's
      campuses participated in this study.

6p   B. Chandrashekhar, K.M. Ganesh, and A. Anantharaman, *"Sri Sathya*
      Sai Water Project: Partnering for MDG", IWP/CR/No.5/2010, Institute of
      Water Policy, National University of Singapore.

6q   Shah, Shashank, *'The Power of Partnership'*, *The Art of Giving*, Business
      India Publications, 2018.

Author's Profile

G ovindarajan Jagannathan, over the years, has been widely known as Jaggu. He has unlocked value for enterprises by his acute sense of excelling in execution. His strategic mind makes sense of the business priorities. His innate ability to execute complex initiatives across vast geography has earned him an adorable reputation to achieve process transformation by implementing quality systems in the two largest companies of the Tata conglomerate. The ability to execute large-scale programmes requires far more than people skills. It requires building relationships with stakeholders and seeing the divinity in people.

His illustrious career spans over 40 years across Steel, Auto, Engineering, IT, Design, Manufacturing, and Quality Management Services. As a senior leader of the $120 billion Tata conglomerate that operates in over 100 countries — Jaggu played a key leadership role in two of its iconic companies by altering its trajectory with business excellence programmes for transformation. He held the position of the CEO of Tata Quality Management Services – a Division of Tata Sons. He later became the Executive Vice President and the Global Head of Business Excellence for Tata Consultancy Services, a $12 billion business that is among the most valuable IT services brands worldwide.

He has worked with partners in Latin America, Europe, South Asia, South Africa, and Australia, gaining a global perspective towards Leadership, Business Excellence, Cost Improvement through Value Analysis and Quality Management.

He has trained thousands of executives worldwide in Leadership, Business Excellence, Value Strategy, and Time Management. He was the CEO of Transconn International LLC, and is currently the Director and Co-Founder of Gurukul Learning Systems.

The Society of American Value Engineers (SAVE), USA, awarded him the Distinguished Service Award. He is a Certified Value Specialist, Fellow of SAVE, Indian Value Engineering Society, IIIE, and IIE. He is the author of two books, *'Getting More at Less Cost: The Value Engineering Way'* and *'The Value Strategy.'*

He holds an Engineering degree from Visvesvaraya National Institute of Technology, a Master's degree in Industrial Management from the Indian Institute of Technology (Madras), India, and an AMP from CEDEP, France.

He lives in Fremont, California, with his wife Lalitha Jagannathan and is blessed with two sons and two grandchildren.

Printed in Great Britain
by Amazon